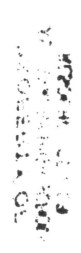

THE

GLOBAL
MYTHS

*Exploring Primitive,
Pagan, Sacred, and Scientific
Mythologies*

THE
GLOBAL
MYTHS

Exploring Primitive,
Pagan, Sacred, and Scientific
Mythologies

ALEXANDER ELIOT

CONTINUUM · NEW YORK

1993

The Continuum Publishing Company
370 Lexington Avenue, New York, NY 10017

Printed in the United States of America

Library of Congress Cataloging-in-Publication Data

Eliot, Alexander.
    The global myths : exploring primitive, pagan, sacred, and
scientific mythologies / Alexander Eliot.
        p.   cm.
    Includes index.
    ISBN 0-8264-0580-0 (alk. paper)
    1. Myth.   2. Mythology.   3. Eliot, Alexander.   I. Title.
BL304.E433   1993
291.1'3—dc20
                                                                        93-3653
                                                                        CIP

For Jane, May, Jefferson, and Winslow,
fellow athletes of the spirit
and Friends at the Rose Cafe

Contents

Part 4: From Eternity to Here   155

Introduction

BY JONATHAN YOUNG, PH.D.

Curator, Joseph Campbell Archives & Library
Pacifica Graduate Institute

Mythology allows us to reconnect with a dimension beyond ordinary time. The ancient narratives provide a stage upon which the great cosmic forces can be seen in human form acting out their vital dramas. The stories reveal that, despite their powers, the mythic characters need each other. We also learn that the interdependence of gods and goddesses extends to mortals. We have a crucial role to play in the unfolding of the sagas.

Not since Joseph Campbell's observations on the power of myth have we been given such a compelling collection of mythic tales. Drawing on a lifetime of explorations through the myths and their landscapes, this book extends Alexander Eliot's marvelous body of work with a series of memorable stories from around the world.

Mythology continually shows us how to align our energies and attention with the forces of the natural world. Eliot assists the reader in this focusing by providing an unforgettable sense of place for each tale, which takes us beyond our particular locales to situate our concerns in the larger world community. Also notable are the animals and trees as active members of the mythic ensemble of players. There are constant reminders that we, too, are animal beings and part of nature, not mere observers. A timeless ecological awareness permeates the mythic worldview.

As in Joseph Campbell's writings, this expansive work draws on a vast spectrum of mythic sources from all continents. As parallels and variations in the tales are recounted, we learn to see the metaphors. Then we can open to an appreciation of the significance underlying every part of the natural and social environment. It becomes clear that the material world has meanings beyond itself.

Every feature of each story is necessary to the whole. The brief appearance of what may seem like an inconsequential maidservant may end up being the turning event of the story. This helps us to enlarge our perceptions to embrace many aspects of life which might be overlooked by a consciousness that is all too socialized. The psychological counterpart is an acknowledgement of the many aspects of an individual personality. The least valued attribute may come to the rescue on some fateful day when that very quality is required.

Alexander Eliot is a master storyteller who evokes the vitality of the immortal characters. The reader feels the presence of the deities of old. In each section, we can see why Joseph Campbell praised the enchantment of Eliot's retelling of age-old stories. Reflections on the tales and insights drawn from decades of scholarship are woven throughout the work. These personal moments are full of wisdom and delight.

In a time of individual and societal troubles, when there is less certainty about familiar guideposts, we may do well to reach back for the timeless wisdom of ancient stories. Every large event, personal or shared, takes us into unfamiliar territory. Mythology helps us to face the best moments and the worst. The gift of mythic vision is that it provides us with maps. We do not have to start from scratch. Bits of guidance have been left behind by those who traveled this way before.

By seeing the global quality of the mythic tales, Alexander Eliot joins such writers as Joseph Campbell and Mircea Eliade in celebrating the common ground that is shared by all humanity. Seeing the great similarities in the world's key teaching stories reveals that living on a shared globe in human form is a kindred experience for all peoples.

Receptive reading of mythology can open up our perceptions

of reality so that a vast web of interconnections becomes evident. In this amazing collection, we find out how to live on this earth. The soul of the planet speaks to us through the mythic imagination.

—Santa Barbara, California
October, 1992

Preface

BY TAITETSU UNNO

Jill Ker Conway Professor of Religion
Smith College

Alexander Eliot's new work is no catalogue of world myths such as undertaken by Eliade or even Campbell, nor is it a doctrinaire pronouncement in the manner of Freud and Jung; rather, he urges each of us to plunge deep into the mythosphere, our own and the world's, and become mythshapers ourselves. In his words: "Simply adding mythic treasure to one's personal store of knowledge does not in itself suffice. We must also imagine our way into myth, as best we can, like actors in a play. If we're not prepared to make that effort, how can we ever fulfill our own roles in the universal drama?" (p. 106). How can we become truly human? How can we truly cherish this life on earth and everything within it?

In retelling stories from his own boyhood, the ancient Greeks, Native Americans, and Taoist adepts, among others, the author opens the Way, so that the reader too may follow his or her own path to the mythosphere. Myth is a liberating consciousness, and because Eliot speaks from the heart of that experience, the choice of his words and the turn of his phrases have in themselves a mythic quality. One is drawn into reading this book at one sitting; the palpable feel of the mythosphere cannot be denied.

Global mythology is especially relevant to our society today, where multiculturalism has become a nasty word in different ways for different people. Although it began with high hopes where we "value all people and all people are valued," it has created more anger, division and mutual exclusivism than anything we have known in recent history. If we can break through the artificial constructs that separate people, cultures, races and religions, the differences highlighted by multiculturalism take on great significance, liberating us from provincialism, enriching our lives, expanding our horizons. Eliot makes this point succinctly: "Sometimes our faiths set us cruelly at odds with one another, true. However, their extreme diversity spells freedom for the human spirit" (p. 47).

This freedom enables Eliot to find the proper niche for art, science, poetry and metaphysics as meaningful, liberating endeavors. Without clashing and denying each other, they celebrate the human spirit containing and contained in the mythosphere. The "Tathagata-garbha" or "Buddha-matrix" invoked by Mahayana Buddhists has a twofold meaning: each of us is the matrix or womb from which the Tathagata or Buddha is born, and at the same time we are all contained in the matrix or womb of Tagatata. Eliot's mythosphere, it seems to me, is an updated version of the Tathagata-garbha that has a tremendous appeal to modern consciousness.

—Northampton, Massachusetts
October, 1992

PART ONE

The House of the Four Winds

Although mortals create myth, relatively immortal myths pervade our lives. The first dimension of existence is physical reality, but we must also deal with psychological reality, economic reality, historical reality—and mythic reality. On the starry nighttime side of human consciousness, myth still lives and reigns. Nothing keeps us from exploring, enjoying, and coming to terms with this mysterious realm. I call it "the myth dimension."

Honor the primal mythmakers of all races, whose names are lost in the mists of time. They pioneered humanity's first great achievement of creative heroism. Whether lofty, luminous, dark, scary, sex-charged, nurturing, or soul-stretching, the stories conveyed by ancestral shamans, witches, and ancient sages still shine through. We can learn a lot in their fitfully gleaming light, but not by applying made-to-order perspectives. A multitude of poets, prophets, priests, parents, performers, and professors have told, retold, compressed, expanded, clarified, obscured, interpreted, and reinterpreted the primal myths in many different tongues all down the centuries. So let's not place too much confidence in Freudian, Jungian, Marxist, or Constructivist theories of myth, let alone racist or sexist interpretations. The whole subject has become far too ambiguous, and too barnacled with exegesis, for dogmatic analysis.

Myth is frustrating to the literal mind and inhospitable to the inhibited. Much of it stimulates and disturbs. All of it shades back into hearsay. There's no strictly "accurate" version of any legend. So one should enter the myth dimension as one embarks upon a love affair. Daringly, that is, in the midst of uncertainty, and yet with a kind of reverence—prepared to face whatever may unfold.

I've had the joy of wandering the world to visit sacred sites and contemplate works of art that open into the myth dimension. Thanks to indulgent publishers plus timely grants from the Guggenheim and Japan Foundations, I've stopped to write on Catalunia's Costa Brava, on a Greek mountainside, in Rome, in Kyoto, and on the edge of England's Ashdown forest—where I composed a compendium of world mythology. And now, during the past few years on the Pacific shore, I've hammered out a celebration of my lifelong love affair with myth. If this can add something to your own adventures in myth dimension, I'll be happy.

Thor in Trouble: Time and Tide

T he Norse thunder-god Thor once found himself in a forest castle belonging to a mist-robed, smiling family of giants. Thor cut through their courteous offerings of hospitality with a boyish challenge. He could, he proclaimed in his downright way, outwrestle anyone around! Thereupon a cackling, toothless old maidservant set aside the tray she was carrying and hobbled across to confront him. The god was about to protest this insult to his powers when she pressed her gnarled fingers to his throat. Thor found himself forced to his knees upon the straw-strewn flagstone floor. The god fought back as best he could. Turning desperate, he even flailed at the maidservant's bony knees with his thunderous hammer, but to no avail.

Like a summer cloud upon a mountaintop, Thor's huge and skeletal opponent stooped darkly over him. Weeping with merriment, gleeful through and through, she never relaxed her grip. It wasn't long before all strength had drained from Thor. Sick at heart and shivering with inexplicable chill, the god signaled his surrender. Snickering, drooling, the ancient creature released him and withdrew.

The giant daughter of the house then rushed to comfort Thor. Cradling him like a helpless doll in her great, smooth, marbly arms, she called for a cowhorn filled with medicinal mead, and set it to his lips. The mead, together with the maiden's musky smell, revived him wonderfully well. Sitting up again and seizing the cowhorn in his fists, he sought to drain the entire potion down. But the more he drank, the more welled up from within the horn!

Manfully, Thor gulped and swallowed pint upon pint. Yet the vessel remained full, while his belly swelled to the bursting-point, and the poor god passed out.

It's said that he awakened on a cold and lonely moor, inhabited by nothing but reindeer. Thor suffered a prodigious hangover, which proved to his own satisfaction that his dream must have been real. Besides, his hammer was dented and bent out of shape. But where had he been, and what had done him in? Was it something tidal? Did it have to do with space and time? Thor asked the Lord of the Unerring Spear, who had given an eye for wisdom. One-eyed Odin replied that in his own experience the giants were a tough lot. Not only that, but difficult to figure out.

I myself once ventured on a lonely hike over the tundra near Norway's North Cape. There, for the first and only time in my life, I encountered a wild reindeer herd. They had come up like soft, sudden thunder over a rise in the rolling and nearly featureless ground. It was hopeless to run. I stood as straight as possible while their tossing velvety horns spun me about and their misty panting breath enveloped me. Naturally, I feared they'd knock me flat; I was terrified of being trampled to death.

Not indifferent to my fate, the animals swerved to right and left as they passed. Within minutes, the whole herd had flowed on out of sight. They left me breathless, staggering, laughing to myself. It was a marvelous experience, since I survived. Perhaps it would have been wonderful anyhow; I don't know.

Wonderful. Marvelous. Things dreamt about, which are also experienced. Real/unreal. Weird. I string these words and phrases together in order to draw a dotted line around what I call living myth, myth as process which plays through our lives. The process is never familiar. Surprise seems part of its very nature. No one ever gets used to the altogether elsewhere, not even when transported there.

"In the Beginning"

What means the distant past, the far future, the divine in nature, the inner existence of plants, the emotions of animals, and the beginnings of mankind? What means our life, our death? And is any sort of immortality in store for us? Tales which purported to convey the truth about such matters were once accepted by whole tribes, cities, and nations, all around the globe. People not only believed in myth, they lived by it. That is, they revered, and were guided by, the central images of their myths. Isn't it the same with us?

Largely unexamined belief-systems provide the basic context of human life in general. We hardly know what myth is all about; that's so, and yet—whether we think we can or not—nobody lives a happy life without the assurances that myth provides. We all trust in science, and most of us practice some religion as well. In short, we live by faith, as human beings must. Spiritually speaking we can't swim; there is no way to breast the unknown on our own. So we are in the same boat with our ancestors!

There was a time when one's own inherited belief system, plus what one learned in school, sufficed throughout life. We have passed that point. Today, our faiths are frayed and our knowledge is discounted. Insistent clamors arise all around. Racial, religious, economic, and political wars abound. Under these conditions, our normal self-assurance ebbs. Society seems bitter turmoil, by and large. We come to feel that little is certain. Yet some things do comfort our minds and pull us together still. Some things help us to maintain our brotherhood, and sisterhood, under the skin. And among all such positive forces, living myth stands first.

Myth used to be regarded as a matter of academic, rather than personal, interest. It was presented in the past tense, as though mythology concerned outmoded accounts of dreamlike and half-miraculous events. In fact, myth is alive and well; it influences all our lives, here and now. That's one thing which psychology has clarified. But myth is not a province of psychology: that doesn't follow. It's true that some psychologists claim professional understanding of myth, on the grounds that it belongs to their particular realm of expertise. Namely the human soul; in Greek: psyche. However, most psyches prove to be so bitter, and/or sweet as the case may be, that the forked, probing tongue of psychoanalysis recoils—numb.

There's nothing wrong with extracting "dream-wishes" or "archetypes" from mythic material. But to dissect and categorize such things with one eye shut, and force the abstruse results to some theoretical conclusion, is useless. Codify myth and in effect you deny it. Accept someone else's codification, and you're in the position of a person who looks up his dreams in a dream-book, hoping to discover what they "signify."

"I do not know what I may appear to the world," Sir Isaac Newton once remarked, "but to myself I appear to have been only like a boy playing on the seashore, and diverting myself in now and then finding a smoother pebble or a prettier shell than ordinary, whilst the great ocean of truth lay all undiscovered before me."

When I was a child I thought as a child, I felt as a child, and so on. I saw things from the corners of my eyes as well as face to face. But now that I've become a man, I find myself peering through dark sunglasses much of the time.

Among my friends in the old days were some red-lettered blocks which I would pile up and then send crashing to the floor again: great fun. And I'm still playing with lettered blocks, in my own fashion. I've never put away childish things, simply transformed them: piling letters into words and words into books. Yet now and then I fear I've lost my way. Worse, that I'll never know the place where I began!

Childhood was more a time of learning than of bafflement. Adulthood is the opposite. Diligently, even angrily, we express, discuss, and defend our ostensibly knowledgeable positions. But little can be decided in this way. Advances are tiny, for two reasons. First, because "my opinion is as good as yours." Second, because under the rules it's possible for me (or anyone) to claim some sort of "expertise," and with it the right to marshal a mind-numbing succession of facts in support of my case. The road to hell is paved with expertise; the life goes out of the party. We come away well-pleased with ourselves, perhaps, but seldom have we taken the least delight in others' efforts. In retrospect, we may complain of having learned nothing new or exciting, nothing that passed beyond mere facts and opinion. We've been chasing our own tales, as Aesop might say.

"In the beginning, was the Word, and the Word was with God, and the Word was God." So opens the Gospel According to Saint John. But the poet Goethe roundly rejected that idea. Goethe's *Faust* says this (in Albert Latham's translation):

> Tis written: 'In the beginning was the word.'
> Already I stick, and who shall help afford?
> The 'word' at such high rate I may not tender;
> The passage I must elsewhere render,
> If rightly by the Spirit I am taught,
> 'Tis written: 'In the beginning was the Thought.'
> By the first line a moment tarry,
> Let not thine eager pen itself o'er-hurry!
> Does 'thought' work all and fashion all outright?
> It should stand: 'In the beginning was the Might.'
> Yet even as my pen the sentence traces,
> A warning hint the half-writ word effaces.
> The Spirit helps me—from all doubting freed,
> Thus write I: 'In the beginning was the Deed.'

That's perfectly in character for Faust. What's more, it fits the modern—scientific—view of things. At the beginning of time, according to cosmologist Stephen Hawking, the entire universe resided in a sort of nutshell. When it cracked wide open to pour forth billion-mile plumes of blazing light, the mother of all shouts must also have occurred. Scientists blithely refer to that as the "Big Bang," and they believe its echo still resounds.

The Yoruba people of Africa tell us that the "Word of Mawu-Lesa" sprayed forth from the Creator's lips to become "The Sons of Fa." The Hindus of India have a different idea. They say the golden vowel "Om" is the immaterial womb of all and everything.

"In the beginning was the Word." The blind Puritan poet John Milton found his voice by listening—in alert uncertainty—for aftertones of the divine. Witness these deathless lines:

> Sweet Echo, sweetest Nymph that liv'st unseen
> Within thy airy shell
> By slow Meander's margent green
> And in the violet embroidered vale
> —
> Sweet Queen of Parley, daughter of the Sphere!

Only if the billion-times-fragmented Word remains part of our human charge—only if we still have a say in it—can we call our souls our own. But sweet Echo has long fled, and the din of present opinion deafens us. Our trouble is not that we "know nothing," it's that we think we know so much. Suddenly the earth swarms with hot information. The intellectual atmosphere turns searingly dry, divisive as hell. Strictly analytical thinking pays off. Wandering, dreaming, and "inviting one's soul" are frowned upon. Too bad.

The gates to the City of Knowledge stand wide indeed, but knowledge isn't everything. If you're looking for inspiration and spiritual elbow-room, then feel along the wall nearby. There you'll discover a low, ivy-covered door. It's unguarded, barely big enough for one person to squeeze through alone. This leads out onto a solitary cliff which overlooks an ocean whose ceaselessly churning depths vibrate with phosphorescent monsters, children of Triton: myths.

The ancient Greeks maintained that although Herakles was dead, he lived. His human body had been burned to ashes, true, but now he was a god. I regard mythology the same way. It's a Triton whose ashes are literature. The godly beast of half-forgotten lore still swims, dives, copulates, and cavorts with his phosphorescent progeny in the timelessness of the sea.

If that sounds metaphysical, it's meant to be. We are bodies, but how much more besides! The same mythic wind and water, the same mythic darkness and light, the same mythic people and animals, live on, ever changing, always reborn. The myths are in the depths, and then again the depths are in the myths. They surface unexpectedly, like fine spume or sparkles on a human soul-wave which comes hissing, lifting, curling under and passing, thousands of years wide.

In his introduction to *The History of English Literature* (1863) Hippolyte Taine observed that "art everywhere is a sort of philosophy made palpable; religion is a sort of poem regarded as true; and philosophy is a sort of art and religion, dessicated and reduced to pure abstractions. Each of these groups centers upon a common element: conception of the world and its origins." Thus, in elegantly gallic style, Taine made the point that art, religion, and philosophy, all three, hark back to the same oceanic murmur. I agree.

Big Fish and Little Fish

E ven in youth, strangely enough, I hungered for classical
art and literature. What didn't occur to me was that we
too are mythshapers, and we also are shaped by myths.
Nor was I aware how far mythology extends beyond the ancient
Greek and Roman arena. Back then, there were two standard
mythologies extant. One was by Thomas Bullfinch, and dated
from the mid-nineteenth century. The other was contemporary,
by Edith Hamilton.

Bullfinch, first, was a proper Bostonian with the soul of a poet.
He lovingly laundered the classic myths to make them suitable
for schoolchildren—no easy task. Although much inhibited, Bullfinch's transcendentalist milieu was richer than our own in at
least two respects. Namely, classical learning and metaphysical
yearning. Can yearning constitute a plus factor? Oh, yes. Consider this poem by Bullfinch's contemporary, Edgar Allan Poe,
who titled it "To Helen," meaning Hellenic culture as a whole:

> Helen, thy beauty is to me
> Like those Nicean barks of yore
> That gently o'er a perfumed sea
> The weary, wayworn wanderer bore
> To his own native shore.
>
> On desperate seas long wont to roam,
> Thy hyacinth hair, thy classic face,
> Thy Naiad airs have brought me home
> To the glory that was Greece
> And the grandeur that was Rome.

Lo, in yon brilliant window-niche
How statue-like I see thee stand,
The agate lamp within thy hand,
Ah! Psyche, from the regions which
Are holy land!

A Boston acquaintance of Bullfinch, Ralph Waldo Emerson, struck an even deeper chord of longing for the realm of myth. Witness these lines from his poem addressed to Dionysus or "Bacchus," the god of wine:

We buy ashes for bread;
We buy diluted wine;
Give me of the true,
Whose ample leaves and tendrils curl'd
Among the silver hills of heaven
Draw everlasting dew;
Wine of wine,
Blood of the world.

—

Wine that is shed
Like the torrents of the sun
Up the horizon walls,
Or like the Atlantic streams which run
Where the South Sea calls.

—

Pour, Bacchus! The remembering wine;
Retrieve the loss of me and mine!

—

And write my old adventures with the pen
Which on the first day drew,
Upon the tablets blue,
The dancing Pleiads and eternal men.

Edith Hamilton sprang straight from the tradition of Emerson and Bullfinch. She also conveyed the supreme values of the classical past with signal success. But things have changed since her day. Regardless of our present shortcomings, we seem far more psychologically aware than our grandparents were. And our sociological horizons have greatly expanded.

To us, mythology no longer means ancient Greek or Roman

legends. It's seamless: a global mystery in which all the black, brown, yellow, red, and white men, women and children of the earth participate. For instance, here's a Navajo narrative to which children of all ages can relate:

As I was walking along through the woods, I met a little bird: Cedar Waxwing. She very kindly hung a string of five flint arrowheads around my neck. Afterwards, I came to the foot of the mountain where the Black Ants live. I watched their games and races for a while. The Black Ant Chief asked what I was doing.

"Just wandering around," I said.

"But where do you come from, my grandchild? It's only proper to tell us."

So I mentioned our home in Whirling Mountain. Thereupon the Chief gave me some white, blue, yellow, and shining herbs to use as medicines. Holding the herbs in my hands, I looked across Black Mountain and saw rain coming down in curtains, threaded with male lightning.

I walked on until, at the crest of a hill, I found a tiny pond. A cornstalk grew out of it, and two eagle feathers floated on its surface. Hoping to grasp the cornstalk as a support while I scooped in the floating feathers, I leaned over the pond from the north. No luck: the cornstalk and feathers alike stayed just beyond my reach. So I tried from the west and then the south, again without success. Finally I tried from the east, lost my balance, and fell in. At once, I found myself swallowed by a huge fish. It descended rapidly, with me in its transparent belly, for no less than four full days and nights.

The first night, we passed Big Reed Place, where the Turtle People congregate. They called out to me, in their silent way, suggesting that I stop with them on my return—assuming I could make it back again. The second night, we passed White Waters Place, where the White Fish People flash and propagate. The third night, we passed Dividing Waters Place, the Water Oxens' stamping-ground. At last, on the fourth night, we reached the home of the Deep Water People.

It was there that I remembered Cedar Waxwing's present: the flint arrowheads. With their help I cut my way out of Big Fish's belly. Then, using the white, blue, yellow, and shining herbs which the Black Ants had given me, I healed the wound I had made. Big Fish was grateful. He remarked that if I'd fallen in from the north side of the pond, Black Fish would have swallowed me. If I'd fallen in from the west, Red Fish would have been the one. While, on the south side of the pond, Blue Fish had been waiting all along.

A crowd of Deep Water People gathered around us. The Deep Water Chief appeared angry at first. "What do you mean," he said to Big Fish, "by bringing an Earth person down to our domain?"

My captor found no reply to this, but luckily a Monster Fish Maiden spoke up for him. A Big Water Fly had whispered the truth in her ear. "This is Holy Boy," she informed the Chief. "His parents are Changing Woman and Great-grandfather Sun."

"Well, why didn't you say so?" The Deep Water Chief proceeded to show me all sorts of secrets which can help the Navajos in time of need.

I came back by a different route. First, mounted on zigzag lightning I paid a visit to the Monster Fish Maidens. Second, I traveled a straight lightning to the Water Horses' home. Third, I cut across on a long rainbow to the Turtle People, who had suggested I stop with them. They gave me some valuable prayer-sticks, and songs as well. Fourth and finally, I climbed a short rainbow to the surface of the pond. With feelings of relief. I clambered out again. From there I soon walked home. My mother, Changing Woman, was ready with a blanket to get me warm.

The Prophet Jonah, too, was swallowed by a monstrous fish. So was Pinocchio, the hero of a relatively modern demi-myth.

Holy Boy's own story seems to plunge me down through a dream to childhood, when I was ten. That summer, my parents banished me to "Camp Mohawk" in the Berkshire Hills. Among our counselors was a large-waisted, middle-aged Sioux Indian who called himself "Chief Little Fish." He seemed kindly disposed, yet glum, and held himself somewhat aloof. That is, until the rainy Sunday, following our obligatory "Nondenominational Christian" service, when I happened upon him in the three-holer toilet behind the boathouse.

"Are you really a chief?" I asked.

"Yes, and a Little Fish."

"Rain always makes me wonder things," I explained.

"Um. When it pours, people start thinking."

This was the first time anyone ever referred to me, even indirectly, as a "person" in my own right. Astounded, I said nothing. After a moment or two, he added: "Weren't you supposed to stay put in Junior Cabin, writing letters home this afternoon?"

"I've already finished my letter."

"That's okay, then. Tell you what. Go round up Billy, Ron, and Red if you like. Say I'll be waiting at Main Lodge, to give you boys some training in cowboy pool."

He taught us pool for an hour or so. Then towards sunset, as the rain tapered off, Chief Little Fish led us out along the pier and lined us up facing westward across the gusty gray lake. "Here's a chant my people sing to Grandfather Sun," he told us, "Listen carefully." The words, in his native tongue, were few and easy to learn. After repeating the chant three times in his deep fuzzy voice he said:

"Now you try, all four boys together. If you get our holy chant correct the first time you sing it, right then the sun will appear!"

Well, we did; and it did, gleaming for a glorious moment through an eye-level rift in the scudding clouds. All this happened a long, long time ago, but I remember it vividly. Sometimes on rainy afternoons I walk down to the beach near my home and perform the prayer again, just as I learned it from Chief Little Fish. For my interior vision, if I may say so, it still works.

Myth, not possessed by anyone, you shelter and inspire everyone.

As Big Fish explained to Holy Boy: if he had fallen in from the north side of the pond, Black Fish would have swallowed him. If he'd fallen in from the west, Red Fish would have been the one. And all the while, on the south side of the pond, Blue Fish had been waiting.

At nineteen, I ran away from civilization—or rather, I drove away, in a Ford V-8. For two glorious summer months I camped alone at various sites on the Navajo and Hopi reservations, an area as large as my native New England.

A distinguished Indian Trader named Hubbell took me in for a time and introduced me to a Hopi wise man. The Hopi let me chauffeur him around on the corduroy dirt roads of that period, first to a wedding and then to a katchina dance. As we drove, the Hopi taught me some simple chants. He also told me enough to change my consciousness, permanently. The impalpable Puritan placenta in which I was born, plus the classically correct cultural bubble in which I'd been educated, simultaneously popped.

Not long after my first visit, Navajo country suffered a severe drought. It's very dry anyhow, mostly desert, so the sheep starved and the people went hungry. Therefore, in their despair, the tribe ceremonially appealed to Holy Boy, whose formal name is "Born of Water." Speaking through various medicine-men, the deity suggested sending a Navajo delegation eastward to Taos. Its mission: to beg for a single cup of water from Blue Lake, which is a sacred possession of Taos Pueblo.

Well, after carefully considering this request, the Pueblo's Elders rejected it. They didn't have one cupful to spare. Looking miserable, the Navajo delegation departed and sloped out of sight down the trail.

Secretly, by night, the Navajos doubled back. Scurrying up the mountainside behind the Pueblo, they reached Blue Lake, scooped up the needed cupful of water, and made off. Soon afterward, the drought hit Taos. Meanwhile heavy thunderstorms blessed Navajo country. The herds revived; the people grew less lean.

I'm talking history. But what's the history behind those events? Let's explore that for a moment.

The Navajos were relatively latecomers to what is now the "Four Corners" region of the southwestern United States. Taos, Hopi, Acoma, Zuni, and other Pueblo tribes had long preceded them. The Pueblo peoples were a chubby and clubby lot. Occupying fairly impregnable clifftop villages, they prospered in the practice of agriculture. To put it bluntly, the Pueblo inhabitants stood centuries ahead of the rootless, bootless, hunting and raiding newcomers. So the Navajos naturally assume that the Pueblo peoples possessed all sorts of secret wisdom, or magic if you will, which they themselves were honor-bound to steal! (The conquering Spaniards, and later still the conquering Anglos, made a very different impression upon the Navajo psyche, so weird and ruthless were they.)

Isn't our situation rather like that of the Navajo Indians when they first lifted their eyes to the Pueblos? We also feel like latecomers, honor-bound to steal a mythic cupful of past magic—as it were, from Blue Lake. Then perhaps our own cultural drought, which Ralph Waldo Emerson already felt (and poignantly expressed in his poem "Bacchus"), will end! The same aspiration murmurs through Edgar Allan Poe's poem "To Helen." On a humbler level, it inspired the mythologizing labors of Thomas Bullfinch and Edith Hamilton, and it's not absent from mine.

Enter, the Mythosphere

Neither a "true myth" nor a "mythic truth" can exist in logic; the terms cancel each other out. However, neither myth nor truth stands alone in the objective sense. Their written texts might be described as objects, but they themselves live only in the earth, the air, the water, and the fire of human consciousness.

In the psyche, as we know, such opposites as true and false coexist very well. Deities do handsprings, witches grow angelic wings, words wobble, emotions turn inside-out and almost every worthwhile thought comes fraught with doubt. Our gears are seldom altogether stripped, and yet the clickety slippage of cognition's cogwheels drives thousands of us crazy every day, and millions more into apathy.

But there's a silver lining, which I call the mythosphere. It resembles the refulgent dome of night by full moonlight, and yet at the same time it's more or less contiguous with our personal craniums. So we could say that it's inside our skins. On the other hand, we sometimes find ourselves in the mythosphere! Lacking its tumultuously fruitful influence, our mental lives would be almost as barren as the moon.

A bookworm twists and turns whereas a butterfly flips and flutters. The steady student of stored knowledge and the aspiring spiritual seeker seem to be opposite sorts. The former may do Readings in the History of Science, for example, while the latter practices Heedings in the Mystery of Silence. Yet both are human; nothing prevents them from incorporating each other's methods. And the best thing for both might even be to try less hard. Then they might witness their own thoughts—not as a hopeless struggle, but rather as a balanced and harmonious process.

In this sense, consciousness resembles breathing, digestion, and so on. It too is a self-contained system yet open at the same time. It's more inclusive than conclusive, more streaming than static, and among its natural functions is the propagation of myth/truth.

Take for instance this question: How did the universe begin? "Genesis," the biblical answer, is elegant, profound, and persuasive enough to inspire very widespread belief. So does the "Big Bang" theory that George Gamow propounded half a century ago and upon which, for the moment, mainstream astrophysicists agree. But these are wildly contradictory versions of events. Moreover, both the biblical and the scientific accounts deal imaginatively with mysteries beyond our ken. Thus they are neither false nor factual; they're myth/truths. In other words, they are courageous, fallible, and yet extremely potent constructs which we men, women, and children, both past and present, help to make real in the mythosphere.

Every man, woman, and child creates myth/truth to a degree. We all participate in the swirling flow of the mythosphere. We do so through a largely unconscious selection process, plus the obscure activity of our own maverick imaginations. Children "make-believe" a lot. We adults also concoct wonderful stories which we half-credit in our hearts. We may even go so far as to develop a few private, personal myths. Yet we can seldom bring ourselves to talk about such things; not even to our closest friends. For fear of seeming "blasphemous" or "unscientific," or "silly" (which is worst of all) we hold our tongues.

That's sad, I think. It happens in part because our youthful efforts to cooperate in the realization of myth/truth are laughed out of court. For instance, if an adolescent in a high-school natural-history class piously refers to Genesis, he or she suffers considerable scorn. That works in reverse as well, when he or she innocently presumes to inject science at Sunday school. Result: the pupil stands insulted, injured, and mentally maimed. Robbed, I mean to say, of what the poet John Keats called: "Negative Capability, that is, when a man is capable of being in uncertainties, mysteries, doubts, without any irritable reaching after facts and reason."

Laboratory experiments demonstrate that a single photon—a vanishingly minute particle of light—can actually pass through two parallel apertures at the same time. It's also true that a single myth shining from the past may invade widely disparate areas of contemporary life and thought, simultaneously.

Again, as in quantum mechanics, myth consists of "waves" and "particles" combined. The "particles" that we encounter in the mythosphere are particular stories, and the "waves" are large-scale, mutually interfering story-clusters which have to do with all humanity's heartfelt concerns. Hence, neither the historical dynamics of myths nor their impact upon present culture can be traced with confidence or systematically plotted. In the mythosphere, alert uncertainty remains a must.

Consider Cinderella with her glass coach and prancing white horses. Or did she really arrive at Prince Charming's party in a yellow pumpkin drawn by a team of mice? One version of her story was collected by a Cantonese mandarin on the jungle shores of the South China Sea, about the year 850. But Cinderella's godmother's wand also points in the direction of Byzantine Court ceremony and ancient Persian marriage customs. Time and retelling in many languages have polished fairy tales like this to an unearthly gleam. They seem to reflect one's childhood along with that of the human race itself.

Such figures as the Princess and the Frog, Sleeping Beauty, or Jack and the Beanstalk return to us (and through us to our children) as intimately glittering half-realities—denizens of ancestral dollhouses. But every now and then, a fairy tale escapes from the dollhouse. It seems to recoalesce at nearly mythic scale, usually because some poet or psychologist has managed to endow it with contemporary relevance.

My own chief concern is with myth as a living whole. It troubles me that the existing maps of this subject exclude both science and the great contemporary religions; they amputate roughly half of our mythic inheritance. Why?

Instinctively, many of us grant "authority" to science. We forget that science-worship goes right against the tentative, self-testing grain of science itself. And we sometimes regard religion as a bugaboo, too "sensitive" for open discussion. That's unconsciously insulting to religionists.

Apart from personal myths and fairy-tale fossils, only four basic myth-types exist. To put this another way, myth blows in four directions. Primitive and Pagan myth comprise the East and West winds of mythology. Sacred and Scientific myth are its South and North winds respectively. These four winds blow from cloudlike continents as it were, each one afloat in a far quarter of the mythosphere. The winds bear many a spicy fragrance along. Their bristling crystal lances glisten with flying foam and flaunt illegibly torn banners of brilliant color. Moreover, these four hugely wheeling winds resound with rhythmic echoes from realms that cannot be directly known.

If ever we turn our faces in a welcoming way to each of the four winds that blow throughout the mythosphere, and if ever we the people demonstrate both curiosity and concern for one another's mythologies, then, but not until then, we shall experience Peace on Earth.

The East Wind:
Bead Woman's Dress

W hat is the power of primitive myth? Bronislaw Mali-
nowski, a pioneering anthropologist, called it "The re-
arising of primordial reality in narrative form." This
class of legend largely concerns human beings in nature, rather
than the nature of human beings. It's unanalytical, intuitive, and
often wonderfully bold—as dreams are bold.

Primitive myth comes to us through the kindness of shamans,
village elders, witches, warlocks, and medicine men. Over the
past hundred years and more, such sources have retold their holy
legends, at least in part, to thousands upon thousands of anthropological field-workers. The resulting literature expands at such a
pace that no single scholar knows more than a small portion of
it. But one can easily cull and re-present this material in such a
manner as to "prove" whatever one pleases concerning human
society and the human spirit.

Whether for career purposes or to promote preconceived ideas,
or simply to make a sharper, more effective impression, specialists
often oversimplify and skew the evidence which mythology offers. Suffice it to note that Sir James Frazer, the titanic author of
The Golden Bough, expressed regret for having led people astray.
He'd never meant to imply that tree-worship and human sacrifice
were all that central to primitive social practice. "Fear of the
Dead," he decided, shaking his snowy locks and scratching his
venerable head, was far more important!

Another thing that interferes with our understanding is this:

when primitive myth is transferred from rhythmic oral transmission to words on paper, it suffers extreme diminishment. Some fur-clad shaman's chant, performed beside the campfire on a cold starry night in a remote region of Turkestan, with drumming and dancing to boot, might well sweep the soul with its cumulative, rhythmic rush. We're not positioned to share in such experience.

If the written record leaves us relatively cold, that doesn't make primitive myths any less holy to the scattered and steadily dwindling peoples who participate in them. And such tribes doubtless keep their profoundest secrets to this day.

It's a little inhuman, I think, to view primitive myth as having merely academic or anthropological interest. If, on the other hand, we approach this subject warmly, in a seeking way, we're practically certain to come upon stories which reconnect us with our ancestors. Wherever one may find them, some few primitive myths appear especially designed to mesh with one's particular psyche. These deepen the world for us. They seem to speak directly out of the dark into your ears or mine alone.

This primitive myth is part of the very rarely performed "Bead Woman Way," a Navajo Indian ceremony. It seems to prefigure Greek tragedy, and science fiction as well. I find the story far and away too subtle to follow, utterly unanalyzable. For that very reason perhaps, it happens to touch my heart:

Bead Woman married a stranger who came from west of the Grand Canyon. They had two sons. One day the elder of the two went out hunting, and disappeared. One year later, to the day, three strangers came to call on Bead Woman's younger son. They'd journeyed all the way from White House Pueblo at Mesa Verde. Their entire tribe, they told the youth, was suffering from acne to an excruciating degree. "It has been whispered that you possess magic powers," they said. "Please come and heal our people. We'll pay you well."

Bead Woman's younger son possessed no magic powers. However, he promised to visit White House during the next full moon. After the emissaries had gone, he sat thinking for a long time. Finally, his elder brother appeared before him and told the following tale:

"When I vanished, it was because the White House People had captured me. For twelve days and nights they kept me tightly bound in their council house. I got nothing but scraps to eat. Then Talking God came to me in dream.

"'Tomorrow,' Talking God said, 'you'll be lowered by rope to an inaccessible rock ledge. There you'll find a nest containing two eaglets, one male and one female. On the plain far below, other White House People will stand looking up, waiting for you to toss down the eaglets. Once you've obeyed, you're finished. You'll be abandoned to starve on the ledge.'

"'Grandfather, this is terrible,' I said. 'What shall I do?'

"'Nothing. Just protect the eaglets.'

"Things happened as Talking God had predicted. Having been lowered to the ledge, I first introduced myself to the eaglets. Fortunately, a Big Fly whispered their names in my ear. All day the White House People on the plain below coaxed me to toss down my new friends. At sunset, the tribe trailed away home, leaving me stranded halfway between earth and heaven. All night the eaglets perched at my sides, warming me with their wings.

"On the second morning, the White House People came streaming back across the plain below. At the foot of the sheer cliff they spread various bribes, including food and drink, in order to induce me to obey. When I still refused, they gave their war cry and began dancing about to frighten me. But my predicament was frightening enough already. On the third morning, the White House People returned again, armed with bows and arrows. Since we were so high up, they shot at us in vain. By now the eaglets had developed to the point where they could fly a little. Circling out from the cliff and back again, they shed a few feathers on our tormentors. Mind you, those eaglet feathers are what spread acne among the White House People.

"Very early on the fourth morning, forty-eight eagles and hawks arrived at our ledge. They'd brought along a turquoise basket and a basket of whiteshell in which to carry the eaglets. Having painted my face with white clay, they gave me a crystal and a hollow reed. Then they wrapped me in a dark cloud, which the crystal lit from inside. When I breathed through the reed it made a whistling sound. The forty-eight hawks and eagles attached three lightning bands and three rainbows to the cloud. They all caught hold of these in their claws. Then, dropping free of the ledge, the forty-eight hawks and eagles soared out and up along the sunrise updraft, bearing me in my dark cloud aloft. Unfortunately, the cloud had a dampening effect upon their beating wings. Four times, the birds were forced to stop and rest upon the air. Finally, feathered serpents looped down from overhead and helped to hoist me up. I found myself drawn through a hole in the sky, to spiritland."

The elder brother had finished his story. He waited politely, but while he was waiting his aspect slowly changed. He became Talking God! This development astonished Bead Woman's surviving son, who nonetheless succeeded in maintaining a semblance of calm. Finally, in a soft voice which shook only a little, the youth spoke up:

"Grandfather, this is terrible. What shall I do?"

"Nothing. Just visit the White House, as you said you would, and heal those people. Now that you know what they did to deserve their acne, it should be easy. Only make sure they pay you as promised. Bead Woman needs a new dress!"

The West Wind:
Laelaps' Last Chase

Pagan myth survives mainly through the Greek and Latin writings of a few incredibly gifted poets. Being symbiotic with classical poetry, it subordinates both the physical and the spiritual words to one's own heart's drama. Friedrich Nietzsche observed (in his seminal essay called *The Birth of Tragedy*) that the Greek gods "justified human life by living it—the most satisfactory theodicy ever invented." Pagan myth generally concerns ironic and tragicomic interactions between human and divine beings. The pagan accent is not on nature, as in primitive myth, but on human nature every time; with the understanding that human nature incorporates something divine.

The Greek and Roman classics undeniably derive from warlike, male-dominated, and uncharitable cultures. They're hard on goddesses, making Hera vindictive and Aphrodite arbitrary. Rape is a staple in pagan myth, and killing still more commonplace. These factors seem especially unsettling to women and children. Men, for their part, tend to shudder at the metamorphoses (changes into fresh life-forms) which animate many a classic legend. Example: the story of Daphne turning into a tree in order to frustrate Apollo's advances.

Even in translation, strange to say, pagan myth is little-read today. Like the languages in which it was born, this seems a lost cause to many. Yet I feel sure the Greek and Latin classics will regain the ground they've lost, because they have so much to give.

Where pagan myth is concerned, no question of anthropological correctness, religious allegiance, or scientific provability occurs. We're free to enjoy the legends conveyed by the ancient Greek and Roman poets precisely because we have no stake in them and don't believe in them. Their sharp, shuddery relevance to our own eternal conflicts shows clear. Pagan myth irradiates the psyche from two directions—reason and emotion—equally. Thus it expands our self-knowledge. There's hardly any greater boon than that.

Ancient Greek literature in general has a quality that ours lacks. It seems predicated upon the conviction that although thoughts are fleeting, they are things. From Homer down through Menander and beyond, Greek poets sculpted what they said, giving it clear-cut shape and weight as well. If a stanza from Sappho, for instance, were to fall on your foot, it might hurt.

Here's a brief pagan myth that speaks to the solidity of the fleeting, and the fleetingness of the solid. Like the tale of Bead Woman's sons, this story too is a personal favorite of mine. It's not happy, either; that doesn't matter. Happy endings are fine, but there's more lasting comfort, as the poet Wordsworth found, in "things too deep for tears."

The heat was great. Even cobwebs wilted. Amphitryon, sweating, leaned on his spear. The grassy ridge where he stood was boulder-strewn and veined with asphodel. Below, a green lake wrinkled wearily, lifting admonitory fingers of mist. The distant baying of a hound tugged at the heavy day.

Laelaps' baying carried well across the lake. It sounded mournful and yet eager, both at once. Amphitryon loved his hound, whom Zeus the Father-god had blessed with indomitable will. This morning it was on the spoor of a rapacious fox, a vixen dear to Hera, supernaturally swift.

The chase grew faint, far out along the water's edge. This would take time, Amphitryon guessed. Setting his spear aside, he sat down on the grass. He wondered if the vixen had a mind to hole up, phantom-like, under the lake. Whatever she did, his hound would run her down. Laelaps could catch any prey.

Like sailors and sentries, hunters also spin long thoughts when they're alone. Dim, fearful thoughts, much of the time. Beyond the mountains, thunder muttered stonily. Amphitryon lay back, dreaming of a scene in heaven. He thought he heard Zeus and Hera quarrelling among the thunderclouds. And then it seemed they called for Hephaestus, the god of artisans, to settle their dispute—whatever it might be about.

Half dreaming, half awake, the hunter heard his hoarse, great-hearted hound. The chase continued and continued on into late afternoon. At last, rubbing his eyes, Amphitryon sat up again. The shadows of the asphodel were stretching out. The boulders appeared bigger than before. The hunt had circled all the way around the lake and back again. Now, just below the ridge where Amphitryon sat, Laelaps' baying resounded—and ceased.

It ceased.

Heat-lightning pulsed on the horizon, molten white. Hurriedly getting up, Amphitryon called his hound. No answer came. With a peculiar shiver of fear, he stooped to retrieve his spear. Straightening, he called again. Not even an echo came. He waited, wondering, clutching his spear. After a time, he strolled down to the darkening lake.

Something like marble gleamed close by the shore, seeming to leap yet not to fall again—a carved statue of a hound! Had that been there before? Leveling his spear at eye-level, Amphitryon sighted along it. Trying to stay calm, he crept up on the statue. Laelaps? He blinked and looked again. How could it be? Hesitantly, he touched the pale flank with the point of his spear, scratching the stone.

In tears, the hunter fondled Laelaps' ears. They too were stone, cold stone, unmoving, unhearing. Angry, frightened at the same time, Amphitryon peered about. A second statue caught his eye. It stood nearby, seeming to lope ahead of Laelaps' silent pursuit. The vixen, cast in bronze, appeared to run with head and brush well down, pads twinkling in the dusk—so quick. Her smooth tongue, gleaming, lolled. Sheer terror shadowed her indented eyes, and yet never would she be caught.

Nor could Laelaps lose her now.

The South Wind:
"Evident Nonsense"

I define as "sacred" the myths which illustrate, adorn, and anoint the living world religions: Hinduism, Buddhism, Judaism, Christianity, and Islam. The core gospels of living religions are mutually exclusive in some degree, which has a paradoxical effect. Sacred myth pulls whole peoples together wonderfully well. At the same time, it tends to divide one people from another. This is deeply troubling to many members of the faiths concerned. It's led others, such as the mystical artist and poet William Blake, to question the authenticity of myth in general.

"The Ancient Poets" Blake wrote, "animated all sensible objects with Gods or Geniuses, calling them by the names and adorning them with the properties of woods, rivers, mountains, lakes, cities, nations, and whatever their enlarged and numerous senses could perceive. . . . Till a system was formed which some took advantage of, and enslaved the vulgar by attempting to abstract the Mental Deities from their objects—thus began priesthood; choosing forms of worship from poetic tales. And at length they pronounced that the Gods had ordered such things. Thus men forgot that All Deities reside in the Human Breast."

Did pre-Homeric bards in the dark backward and abyss of time create "poetic tales" that later came to be matters of faith? It's possible. Does Blake's romantic scenario also apply to presentday religions? That runs right against orthodox doctrine. The Bible and the Koran, for example, are claimed to be the Word of God—"revealed," or even "dictated" to historic personages. Is this how it was? If so, in how many cases does the formula hold good? Ecumenically inclined theologians welcome such hard questions. However, the fundamentalist faithful everywhere maintain that their gospels were divinely inspired—and competing texts not.

I respect the importance, for religion and philosophy alike, of hard and fast distinctions. To me, however, the dividing line between "divine revelation" and "human inspiration" appears to be written in disappearing ink. The important thing is this: whether sacred myth be regarded as human, or divine, or both combined, it sustains and in some degree sanctifies the vast majority of human lives.

Nothing prevents us from approaching religions which are not ours in an open-hearted manner. When one applies temporary "suspension of disbelief" to the *Baghavad Gita,* the *Diamond Sutra,* the Book of Job, the Revelation Given to John, or *The Night-Journey,* for example, one's sense of the universal nature of sacred myth is confirmed and its enduring shock value rays through. To scoff at Vishnu, Buddha, Jehovah, Christ, or Allah, is to mistake the bread of life itself for stones. True, those deities reside "in the human breast," as Blake put it, but that is by no means their only place of residence. In music, art, architecture, and so on, they make their presence felt. In holy services, prayers, and good works, they move and breathe all around us.

How questionable is somebody else's personal experience at the deepest level? I'll put that another way: is it proper to doubt someone else's religious faith? Ordinary tact suggests the answer: not very, that is, if you wish to be friends. Yet, toward the end of his life, the eminent mythologist Joseph Campbell took a surprisingly tough stance on this one. In *The Inner Reaches of Outer Space,* Campbell deplored:

> The interpretation of mythic metaphors as references to hard fact: the Virgin Birth, for example, as a biological anomaly, or the Promised Land as a portion of the Near East to be claimed and settled by a people chosen by God, the term "God" here to be understood as denoting an actual, though invisible, masculine personality, who created the universe and is now resident in an invisible heaven to which the "justified"

will go, when they die, there to be joined at the end of time
by their resurrected bodies. . . . What, in the name of Reason
or Truth, is a modern mind to make of such evident nonsense?

The encyclopedic philosopher Mortimer Adler takes issue with
that. In a book called *Truth in Religion,* Adler comments that
Campbell's "competence in dealing with philosophical matters,
especially in the field of philosophical theology, is highly questionable. His judgment in this area reflects the dogmatic materialism that is so prevalent in contemporary science, especially in the
behavioral sciences."

Like Campbell, however, Adler also drapes himself in the soiled
ermine of Western "Reason." Dismissing both Hinduism and
Buddhism, Adler argues that only three religions—Judaism,
Christianity, and Islam—possess legitimate claims to what he calls
"logical truth" and "factual truth." In Adler's opinion, even these
three faiths could use a good scrub-up to disabuse the "supersti-
tious" common folk:

> Take for example, the New Testament story of the three
> wise men who came from the far corners of the earth bringing
> gifts to attend the nativity of Jesus of Bethlehem; and the Old
> Testament stories of the flood and Noah's Ark, and of the
> Tower of Babel. . . . For those who . . . accept the stories as
> factual history rather than as fictional narratives, the removal
> of their self-deception can only come from showing them how
> to interpret the texts correctly, in a nonliteral manner.

Adler goes on to propose a summit symposium, presumably
with himself as moderator. He "would like to hear the leading
twentieth century theologians speaking as apologists for Judaism,
Christianity and Islam engage in a disputation. . . . It being con-
ceded that each has a claim to some measure of truth, which of
the three can rightly claim more truth than the other two?"

In short, let's see whose priests make the best professors. But
religion does not reside in theological abstracts. Whether they be
Jewish, Christian, Islamic, Hindu, Buddhist, or whatever, religions don't depend upon "disputation" or "apologetics" because
the mythosphere makes room for all. Neither "logical truth" nor

"factual truth" is at issue there. Faith rests upon another kind of truth altogether: myth/truth, as I call it.

Stammering, shimmering, shrouded in mystery, religious gospel echoes and re-echoes with unearthly cries of the violently stretched mind, the burning heart. That's why, when they were first proposed, the teachings of most saints and prophets were thought to be subversive, not to say heretical. Borne upon south winds of the sacred, which blow wherever they may wish to do so, great faiths come and go.

Sometimes our faiths set us cruelly at odds with one another, true. However, their extreme diversity spells freedom for the human spirit.

The North Wind:
Dancing in the Dark

Religionists say, in effect: "God told me; this is how it is." Scientists argue: "The relevant data arrayed itself before me and showed me; this is how it is." In both cases, objectivity is claimed. But moderns grant the claim most readily to science. There are two reasons for this. First, the work done along the lower scientific slopes is resolutely factual. The foot soldiers of science (particularly technologists) prove extraordinarily useful more often than not. Second, and more importantly, science appeals to observation plus reason. It excludes emotion. There lies its convincingness—its cold yet genuine comfort.

Most of us can think more or less unemotionally when we bend our wills to that. It's rather like learning to drive a car. Unlooked-for freedoms, including speed, result. Glancing at the dashboard instruments, we assert without a smile: "To measure is to know!" Eventually, however, numbness sets in, followed by delusions of grandeur, plus ice-palaces built in the brain, and before we know it we've skidded off the road again.

Science has long been of prime practical importance to civilization as a whole. Yet the most solemn and revered creeds of science—from Lucretius on Nature through Darwin's "The Origin of Species" to Erwin Schrödinger's Cambridge lectures—are imagination-powered. This, plus their extreme boldness, originality, and persuasive power, justify our calling them scientific myths.

"The history of science, like the history of all human ideas, is a history of irresponsible dreams, of obstinancy, and of error. But science is one of the very few human activities—perhaps the only one—in which errors are systematically criticised and fairly often, in time, corrected." So the philosopher Karl Popper declared, with sputtery vehemence, at a 1960 conference. Popper was of course aware that science, like religion, comes burdened with heavy chains of precedent plus "vested interest." Biotechnicians and parish priests alike must live with that.

Still, by hook or by crook, science and religion alike progress—albeit, they meander. The basic appeal of science lies not in particular theories but in its ongoing intellectual adventure. For instance, Ptolemy's depiction of the cosmos lasted fifteen centuries, only to be disproved by Copernicus and demolished by Isaac Newton. Then along came Albert Einstein, who outstripped Sir Isaac at a walk, saying: "Watch my stardust!" But will Einstein's theory prevail forever?

Meanwhile, it's not too much to say that scientific myth weaves the backdrop of modern existence. There's no reason to deny it or to deplore it either. Science invites our critical participation at best, and our basic appreciation at the very least. By providing such support, we challenge the deterministic view that humans will never understand, let alone control, their destinies.

Basic science reflects thousands of careful observations which have been incorporated in reams of numerical analysis and accordioned together, so to speak, on the assumption that relations between numbers strictly parallel relations between things. The assumption seems reasonable; is it always so?

The philosopher Scott Buchanan once observed in conversation that science resembles theater. What happens to an atom in an atom-smasher and the hero in a Greek tragedy, he explained, are identically unclear. That's because the action in both cases remains "allegorical." Neither one offers anything more solid than a system of analogies.

In *The Structure of Scientific Revolutions,* Thomas S. Kuhn carried that curious train of thought to its logical conclusion. Namely, that science lives by "paradigms" or temporary allegorical umbrellas of shared belief. Propositions must never be regarded as "true," or "false" either, Kuhn contends, except within the context of a particular paradigm—such as quantum theory.

Like most people, I stand amazed by the reach of physical science. Again, like most people, I'm troubled by its implications for humanity. Modern cosmology implies that this planet and all its creatures, including us, amount to little more than a spitball such as one surreptitiously flicked at school. Life is an exiguous accident, we're told, and death a tiny splatter in the boundless, totally uncaring ocean of energy/matter. That's disturbing, all right. However, it's no excuse for dismissing modern cosmology.

> During the very earliest stage of the Big Bang, a period that lasted only a million trillion trillionth of a second and ended when the universe was about the size of a softball, there was an extremely rapid expansion-rate—a rate a billion trillion times faster than the speed of light.

That mind-boggling snippet of astrophysical theory concerns "the beginning of time." It's what sparked these cogent comments in *The Boston Globe* by science pundit Chet Raymo:

> Imagine! A universe the size of a softball, expanding a billion trillion times faster than light! The lickety-split softball contained as pure energy everything that exists today—the billions of galaxies we observe in our telescopes, each galaxy containing hundreds of billions of stars, many of those stars whirling a family of planets, planets (for all we know) crackling and popping with life. . . . We're talking about something the size of a softball figuring out what happened to the universe when the universe was the size of a softball. Got it?

While pressing one's nose to the darkened shop window of the unknown, one is likely to find one's own peculiar cast of mind reflected in the glass. Thus, a religionist may envision angels dancing merrily on the head of a pin, whereas a scientist may swear that sheer numbers appear to him or her—leaping through zero hoops from positive to negative and back again. Now, providing that their personal experience of the case is genuine, wouldn't it be a mistake to regard either believer as "mistaken"?

Having ballooned safely outward for fifteen billion years, as one assumes, how do things appear at our own parlous point in time? If it's a clear night, take a look. The stars are extremely distant, for sure. This hardly keeps them from twinkling, like laughter in heaven.

Scientific myths are valid while they last, very nearly as influential as sacred ones. We have every reason to be grateful for both sorts, as well as for pagan and primitive myth. These four myth-types, along with fairy tales and personal myths, constitute a luminous although self-contradictory miracle: namely, the mythosphere—thousands of years in the making—as it exists today in my psyche and yours.

· PART TWO ·

The Labyrinthine Ways

An artist named Len Lye, whose genius may be recognized someday, once invited me to witness the birth of a new creature—nonmaterial—in his studio. First, Len set a tall tensile-steel rod bolt-upright in an electrified black-box pedestal. Then, he flicked a switch and stood well back. African drums played as the rod shivered out of sight. Soon it reappeared, dancing, invisibly shaping fugitive arcs of light—like sword-play in the half-darkened room. "That was awesome," I said afterward. "What does it signify?" Len replied indirectly by relating a prehistoric myth which goes like this:

"A lion, an elephant, a gazelle, a monkey, and a man, were friends. They used to sleep side by side in a cavern. When one of them turned over in bed, the others did the same. But after some time, the man began getting up in his sleep, standing straight, then lying down again on his other side. The others were disturbed by his behavior, but they tolerated it. However, the man himself decided not to stay. One morning, regretfully, he waved goodbye to his friends and walked away, upright, out of sight."

Scientific myth has much in common with primitive mythology worldwide. Indeed, the idea that humans are curiously evolved cousins of the animals seems basic to primitive myth in general. Len's legend came from Africa, appropriately enough, since most anthropologists regard that as the womb-continent of humanity.

Having named the four quarters of myth—Primitive, Pagan, Sacred, and Scientific—the tidy thing would be to devote a separate section to each one. But they mix and blend, as in Len's legend. The relatively vast Primitive and Pagan mother-lode en-folds later Sacred and Scientific lore in a matrix of mystery. Hence, I've elected to cut the cake another way. Part Two of this book deals primarily with Knowledge, Part Three with Imagination, and Part Four with Compassion.

A-maze-ingly elaborated circuits of knowledge, such are the "Labyrinthine Ways." They consist in monumental meanders, or walled paths, which wise men and women, both ancient and modern, construct for us to follow. These paths go winding into physical, psychological, and historical realms, all three. Thus they often intersect what mystics call "the Way." But that is a single path, yours alone.

Holy Breath

The ancient Syrian sage Iamblichus maintained that certain statues should be worshipped as gods. He argued as follows:

> The human soul, when filled with deity, energizes about it. Hence, in consequence of energizing above its own power, it becomes weary. For it would be a god, and similar to the souls of the stars, if it did not become weary. However, a sacred statue, conformably to its participations, remains illuminated.

Something in my present line of vision was carved with the express purpose of "energising about" deity. It's a small, primitive object, with a Stone Age background. I'm looking at a stone fox, small enough to palm. The talisman grins from its loping position on my bookshelf. Highly polished, inlaid with a bit of turqoise, it's a "fetish," or semi-sacred stone. Here's the Zuni myth explaining how such objects first sprang into existence:

> In the Days of the New, when Father Sun sent his twin children down to lead us out from underground, the world was still wet and unstable. Our footprints filled with water as we walked. So the Holy Twins shot lightnings across the earth, to dry it. And wherever the Twins encountered a giant beast of prey, they used lightning to petrify and shrivel it down. Thus were the animal tribes brought into balance with us relatively helpless folk.
> And the Holy Twins addressed the beasts which they had transformed into stone, saying: "That you may not do evil unto men, but rather aim them on their way, have we changed you to

rock everlasting. Your holy breath, preserved within the stone, shall guide and comfort our people for ages to come."

Bathed in the holy breath and turquoise grin of my fetish, I smile respectfully. I'm forever grateful to the oppressed but not depressed Native American sculptor Albenita Yunie, who created this. Who am I to deny the power of the carved pebble on my bookshelf?

The Tale of Tarantula

F rank Hamilton Cushing was an unsung hero of American
ethnology. In 1879, at age 22, he took part in an expedition
under Major John Wesley Powell, a famed explorer of the
Western Frontier. The people of Zuni Pueblo seemed mere savages
to Cushing's cohorts, but the youth fell in love with them. At
his request, he was "posted" to the Pueblo as a resident ethnologist. The Zuni treated him as a guest. Over the following five
years, Cushing learned the language, mythology, and rituals of
his hosts. They in turn adopted him into their Macaw Clan and
made him a practicing "Priest of the Bow." In the myth dimension, he became one of them.

Cushing translated many legends told by the Zuni. Here's one
concerning a manlike old tarantula and a radiant youth called
"Swift-Runner," who used to dash right around Thunder Mountain every morning:

Tarantula would sit at the entrance to his hole under the mountain, enviously watching Swift-Runner flash past. One day he
called out: "Hold on, my friend; come over here!"

"Why should I? I'm in a hurry, you know."

"Wouldn't you like to see how fine you look today?"

"Yes, but it's not possible."

"Just take off your things. I'll put them on, to show how beautiful you are!"

That struck Swift-Runner as an excellent idea. Sitting down,
he kicked off his painted moccasins, one red and one green. Then
he removed his whiteshell anklets, his fringed white cotton leg-

gings, his embroidered cotton shirt, his long turquoise earrings, and finally his beautiful macaw-feather headdress. Gaily he tossed each item of clothing to Tarantula, who slipped them on.

"Well, how do I look?" Standing up straight on his bow-legs, Tarantula backed away towards his hole.

"It's a beautiful costume—" Swift-Runner began, diplomatically enough. At that moment, Tarantula turned around and plunged headfirst out of sight.

Naked, dark with misery, the youth trudged home. He told his tribe what had occurred. Angrily, the people rushed to dig Tarantula out of his hole and recover Swift-Runner's costume. All day, they excavated the sand around the hole, until at last they reached bedrock. But Tarantula's hole continued on down into the rock itself, so he escaped them.

Next morning they sent a kingfisher, an eagle, and a falcon, each in turn, to try and snatch Tarantula's stolen clothes. But the sly one has eyes with many sides. He saw each bird coming and ducked back down his hole. There, all alone in his dark deep room of rock, Tarantula danced a jig. Prancing, fluttering his bright stolen garments, he sang nonsense words in a high, wheezing voice:

> "Ohatchikya ti takwa.
> Ai yaa takwa!
>
> Ohatchikya ti takwa
> Ai yaa takwa!"

Swift-Runner meanwhile went on pilgrimage to the mountain gods. Could he ever recover his sunny costume? "You can do it," the gods told him. "Just tempt Tarantula into leaving his hole to hunt!" Thereupon they presented Swift-Runner with two deer and two antelope, animals which they had shaped from powdered rock. Swift-Runner drove the magical beasts in the direction of Tarantula's hole, singing as he went:

> "Here come deer and antelope.
> Here come deer and antelope!

Whoever's near should have good hope
Of shooting deer and antelope!"

In the depths of his hole, Tarantula harkened to Swift-Runner's song. Hunting and killing were his chief joys in life, so now he snatched his weapons and scrambled up into daylight to see what was what. The deer and the antelope had already drifted past! Loping hotly after them, he shot off four arrows in swift succession. All four animals fell dead. Gloating, Tarantula prepared to drag home his prey. But as he did, so the animals became heaps of rock!

Sensing that he'd been tricked, Tarantula turned and scurried back towards his hole—too late. Swift-Runners' tribe had surrounded the entrance. Roughly seizing Tarantula, they stripped off his bright clothing and gave it back to Swift-Runner. Then they cast Tarantula into a bonfire.

How the sly one squeaked, howled, sizzled, hissed, and swelled his hairy carapace! Finally, with a terrific noise, he burst into a thousand pieces! The billowing smoke of the bonfire swirled those fragments far and wide over the earth. Tarantula is immortal, as we know. His scorched, cindery residue lived on and multiplied, becoming the tarantulas of today.

On the cosmic plane, that story concerns the shortest days of the year—our Christmastime or Chanukah—when the sun goes furthest south and loses its full blaze of glory for a spell. But there's a social plane to the myth as well. It teaches wariness and points to the danger of narcissism.

From a modern perspective, Tarantula's initial ruse against Swift-Runner seems almost a caricature of psychoanalytic practice. Psychiatrists also encourage self-stripping on the part of their patients. Then, at each session's appointed end, they plunge head-first, in satisfied silence, from sight.

"Carry on running!" That's what the Zuni elders still inculcate. "Don't let self-concern draw you off your allotted course." It's true that some myths inspire strategies of self-fulfillment. But many more point the opposite way. "Don't examine your impulses," they say, in effect. "Beware of temptation; obey the rules."

For us today, neither self-fulfillment nor self-sacrifice will do. Our goal is to find a third way, both reverent and free.

Terrible Twins: Psychology

The interaction of opposing pairs such as heat/cold, tension/repose, or positive/negative electric charges, proves very useful for technology and experimental science. When forcibly split, subatomic particles sometimes turn into twins which seem to mirror each other's trajectories at astonishing distances. Mathematical equations, too, are a kind of twinning.

The Symplegades or "Clashing Rocks" were natural features, twins of an impersonal sort. Once upon a time, according to pagan lore, the Symplegades actively guarded the straits of the Euxine Sea. They stood a good ten yards apart, yet every few minutes those beetling cliffs would grate grindingly together, like the winking of a granitic needle's eye. No ship could thread the passage until finally Jason's hard-rowing Argonauts managed to pull through in time. As the epic *Argonautica* by Apollonius of Rhodes relates, Jason's vessel lost her tail-ornament, or poop-adornment (or should I say the tuft of her aft?), in that adventure. Thereafter, the Rocks clashed no more.

The warlike West African "People of the Fon" say that twin serpents, one male and one female, twine exactly seven thousand coils about the earth to keep it energized. We glimpse their scaly coils in the glitter of the stars. Also in rainbows, where the red-orange glow of the male serpent and the blue-green gleam of his female twin arch gloriously up and over, blending together, joined in sexual ectasy.

That stunning concept parallels some admittedly far-out astrophysical speculation of the present time. This concerns billion-mile serpents of positively and negatively charged "dark matter."

Although invisible to present probes, such preternaturally potent super-snakes are conceivably copulating throughout the icy blackness of outer space. The calculations of Eric J. Lerner, among other cosmologists, suggest that, yes, such serpentine, electromagnetic entities maintain the universe.

The idea that twin serpents pour energy, life, and health—together with some corrective poison—into our world, also survives in a popular medical emblem: the so-called "caduceus." The caduceus was once a heraldic wand which the Greek messenger-god Hermes carried. It consists of an upright staff with twin snakes twined lovingly around it.

In pagan lore, the twin children of Nemesis threatened to pile Mount Ossa on top of Mount Pelion and pull down Zeus himself! His daughter Artemis saved the day, but barely. When the twins were out hunting, she ran between them in the form of a ravishing doe. The twins cast their whistling spears from either side, transfixing each other.

The Orinoco Indian pantheon includes twin savior-deities: Iureke and Shikiemona. This mischievous pair turned their fire-swallowing Toad foster-mother into a stew—which they then served up to their Jaguar foster-father. Afterward, they assumed cockroach form and pestered the poor fellow throughout his lonely meal! When he learned how he'd been tricked, the Jaguar swore to revenge himself upon his foster-sons by eating them for dessert. Weeks passed, however, while he searched in vain for the twins. Then one fine day, the Jaguar found Iureke and Shikiemona swinging on a vine which dangled from a very tall palm tree.

"What do you think you're doing?" he roared.

"We gain power this way," Iureke told him. "Won't you try it?"

"Well, I could use more power now, and eat you fellows later." So saying, the gullible beast twined himself in the vine. Iureke gaily pushed him so that he swung high, high up and out—while Shikiemona cut the vine. The Jaguar is reported to have crashed in a distant country, mad as hell.

Mythology and psychology also slide together, twine and part, joust and join again. Sigmund Freud and Carl Gustave Jung are mythopoeic twins in their own right, wise men of old whose mysterious powers still steep the intellectual world. Like Iureke with the Jaguar, Freud persuaded us to climb a vine called sex-consciousness, set us swinging, and gave us a great push. Then Jung, like Shikiemona, chopped the vine in half to send us flying. It's possible that we haven't yet returned to earth.

"Follow your bliss!" Joseph Campbell proclaimed that simple program for personal fulfillment. The implication: one does well to regard oneself as a legendary figure. True?

To emulate the goatherd of fairy tale, who answered three riddles and won the hand of the king's daughter in marriage, may be harmless enough. To take father-murdering, mother-marrying Oedipus for a model would be something else again. Let alone following in the footsteps of Herakles or Medea—both of whom destroyed their own children. Actually, a significant proportion of mythological heroes and heroines became human sacrifices—willingly or otherwise. But Campbell seems to have been talking about daydream activity. In his first broadly influential book *(The Hero with a Thousand Faces)* he explained that daydreaming combined with psychoanalysis can be extremely helpful:

> The dangerous crises of self-development are permitted to pass under the protecting eye of an experienced initiate. . . . The doctor is the modern master of the mythological realm, the knower of all the secret ways and words of potency. His role is precisely that of the Wise Old Man of myths and fairy tales whose words assist the hero through the trials and terrors of the weird adventure. He is the one who appears and points to the magic shining sword that will kill the dragon terror, tells of the waiting bride and the castle of many treasures, applies healing balm to the almost fatal wounds, and finally dismisses the conqueror back into the world of normal life.

Campbell's testimony once lulled the doubter in me. Then I remembered that psychiatrists are human, fallible as the rest of us. Moreover, psychological theories are just that: theories. Beware the Clashing Rocks, or tuck in the tuft of your aft at least! At a recent conference on psychotherapy, Mary Watkins rather acidly stated:

> Each culture constructs a . . . model of selfhood that it takes

for granted and assumes to be universal or preferable. These constructions are reflected both in the kinds of suffering people experience and in the culture's modes of healing. In its efforts to understand the self, psychology—itself a cultural artifact— has often failed to see through the assumptions and values that its theories of self are based upon.

Dr. Watkins represents a new, self-critical movement among professionals, one which may yet rescue psychiatry from the dead hands of titans past.

As everybody knows by now, Sigmund Freud identified the "sex-drive" as the prime motivating factor in human behavior. He had something there, by the tail as it were, if not the entire animal. Freud also maintained that dreams, fixations, hysterical attacks, madness—and myths—are efforts to evade, disguise, project, or otherwise disempower the dark, dangerous, sex-based impulses which cry up out of our unconscious selves, tearing us to pieces.

It's not too much to say that Freud captured and transformed cultivated thought, casting a new conceptual vocabulary, netwise, over previously unsuspected reaches of our mental interiors. The tragic drama which Sophocles derived from the Greek myth of Oedipus, Freud declared, keeps being acted out around the world, forever. It represents the one and only fundamental urge at the heart of all human suffering! As he explained:

"King Oedipus, who slew his father Laius and married his mother Jocasta, merely shows us the fulfillment of our own child-hood wishes."

Quick, when you were little, did you passionately yearn to murder one parent and also make love to the other? If not, it's possible that Freud was wrong; the myth of Oedipus may not mask a universal desire. However, Freud was a great writer and a compelling personality. He elaborated his fundamental assertion in subtly poetic and yet seemingly scientific fashion, with aston-ishing success.

Carl Gustave Jung, Freud's favorite disciple, was hailed by the master as a spiritual son and heir. They fell out when the younger man "betrayed" Freud's leading idea by adding an equally weird one of his own. Jung decided that the individual "Unconscious" posited by Freud contains an inner oligarchy which the master failed to notice. Universal, impersonal, and identical in all human beings, this hidden oligarchy makes its presence felt by means of myths, dreams, and "free associations" in one's head. It reigns over a hitherto unguessed mental soul-pool which Jung dubbed "the Collective Unconscious." And it's made up, he said, "of pre-existent forms, the Archetypes."

The Archetypes, Jung proclaimed, are daemonic figures, genetically transmitted, everywhere the same, throughout the human race. Jung named his new discoveries "Anima," "Animus," "Shadow," "Wise Old Man," "Cthonic Mother," etc. They're the ruling body in every single psyche; no exceptions allowed. Jung invariably "discovered" the same few figures sitting within each and every patient's mind—like Swiss cuckoo clocks on a shelf. Whoever dared to deny the Archetypes, the doctor warned, was "in their hands, just as a typhus epidemic flourishes best when its source is undiscovered."

How's that for chutzpah? The doctor's "Wise Old Man" Archetype suspiciously resembles Jung himself. And Jung's therapist heirs don't hesitate to assume the Wise Old Mantle. As for Jung's most appealing and popular Archetype, the "Anima" seems basically an inspirational figment modeled on the muse-figures of classical poetic convention. As it happens, I'm for that. But in Jung's doctrine, only males are entitled to invoke a female muse or "Anima." If you're a creatively inclined woman, the doctor insisted, then you must call upon the "Animus" instead. Now according to Jung, the Animus operates as a not-nice, all-male editorial board somewhere inside your fluffy head!

Both Freud and Jung sought wisdom in mythology. Each man seized a classic portion of humanity's mythic inheritance and bent her, penetrated her to the womb, with their masculine theorizing powers, not to mention personal desires.

Jung flourished as the aging Freud's equal—and worst enemy. Both men wield wonderful, not to say mythic, influence to this day. They were intellectual liberators, triple-threat men gifted with soaring imaginations, glowing charisma, and literary genius. However, the so-called case histories which they composed with such artistic aplomb prove nothing. We owe respect to these illustrious twin figures, who cast such a long double-shadow across the twentieth century, but not for their so-called "scientific" achievements. They were jealously ambitious mythmaker-poets, disguised as doctors in white tunics.

Io's Legend:
Cause for Debate

Princess Io strolled alone beside the Lernian spring, picking raspberries here and there, delighting in the prickly ripe taste of each one, while mist descended from the mountain escarpment at her back. She'd been sweating before, but now she shivered as the mist enveloped her, flowing over her limbs like wet cold wool. Io panicked; she ran until she lost the path, then made herself halt and catch her breath. At that point, a pale pocket in the mist opened before her. From it stepped a very large, virile and kingly figure. He was nude, radiant, terrifying in his obvious excitement.

"Do you know me?" he asked complacently.

Io pretended ignorance.

"No need to be afraid. I'm hardly a beast of prey. Not like the lynx whose piss lies at your breast!"

"What on earth do you mean, sir?"

He pointed. "That carbuncle pin. Don't you know that after seven days a lynx's piss will set and turn to carbuncles? The lynx is a mean, selfish creature. That's why he scratches dust over his piss, to conceal it."

She had to smile a little.

"Some kings are like that also," Zeus went on. "For example, your dad has kept you hidden far too long. This afternoon, I'll make you a woman!"

"Wait. Don't hurt me. Instead, show that you're not cruel and unjust!"

"How's that again?"

"Release Prometheus, the friend to man, whom you keep crucified upon a far Caucasian peak!"

Zeus frowned, a chilling occurrence:

"Listen, child. In the first place, Prometheus stole fire for you
people. Burnt offerings make my nose tickle. In the second place,
he invented fishnets, a cruel device whereby innocent fish leap
weeping to your frying pans. In the third place, he helped you to
tame horses. Today the better animal wears a bridle and bit, while
the worser casts a cold, conceited eye. In the fourth place, Prometheus armed you with spears; since then you skewer each other
self-righteously. In the fifth place, he taught you to build with
stone, whereupon you crowned Arcadia with headache towns. In
the sixth place, he dreamed up the wheel, and ever since then
you've been creating ruts for yourselves. In the seventh—"

The mist was burning off. Io laughed aloud with relief. "Your
wife is coming! Look over there."

"Great Balls of Uranus!"

Where Princess Io had stood a moment before, nervously fin-
gering her carbuncle pin, a white heifer gleamed in the returning
sunlight. The cow's mild brown eyes were moist with unspo-
ken reproach.

"Look, my dear," Zeus called gaily. "Isn't this a lovely heifer?"

Majestic, robed in blue, the bride of Zeus floated down to in-
spect the animal. Thoughtfully, Hera pulled a tuft of clover from
the ground and offered it.

Lifting her pink muzzle in piteous protest, Io refused the treat.

"This is no ordinary heifer," Hera said lightly. "The bulls
shouldn't be at her yet. So if it's all the same to you, I'll take the
pretty beast in charge."

Io's consciousness had been confused and rendered dreamlike
by the fact that she was now a cow. She received the impression
that the Queen of Heaven ordered a monster named Argus to
guard her well. Argus looked like tarry smoke and sparks, an
earthblown tatter of deep space. Between the dark shaggy locks
of his head, more than a hundred eyes blinked and blazed. But
now a second figure—Hermes, messenger of Zeus—appeared in
Io's dream.

Hermes was playing his flute, so beautifully that the eyes of Argus winked out, one by one, in blissful oblivion. Now Hermes lifted up a double-bladed axe and brought it down again with a dull snicking sound. The lopped head of Argus nosed, listening still, into the silver dust. Io stood free. Resignedly, she guessed that Zeus would soon appear to change her back into a girl again. Well, she could live with Zeus' lust, but no such luck. Instead, the jealous Queen of Heaven sent a gadfly.

As cruel as it was small, the insect drove Io the white cow for mile after mile. Lurching, snorting, bellowing with pain, she ambled westward over the Molossian wilderness to Dodona, where the wind in the oak trees whispered distant endearments of Zeus. Northward then the gadfly hurried her, along the edge of sea which has ever since been called "Ionian." Blisteringly, the gadfly then drove Io down the Danube valley, far out across the Scythian plateau, and southward again into the Caucasus—where she was granted pause to glimpse Prometheus on his peak.

Spitting icicles and weeping tears of frost, the crucified one wrenched at his adamantine bolts. With the wind in his snowy beard, the Titan shrilly declared:

"Horned Io, mild of eye, now hear Prometheus prophesy. Never can a savior save himself, for all he gave. But your great-great-grandson is destined to rescue me!"

"Will he be human?"

"Partly."

"Will I myself ever regain human form?"

"That's not the point. Your present wanderings, in the guise of a cow, are purely symbolic!"

"What?" Io could hardly believe her hairy ears.

"My crucifixion is symbolic, too. Never mind the pain. It stands for poetic justice, you understand. In other words it's what I get for trying to bring some semblance of scientific law and order into a sex-crazed, chaotic world."

"I thought Zeus did this to you."

"Zeus, you say? Never heard of him. . Oh, why can't things ever stand still and make sense for people? They do for me."

"But not for me! Why must I suffer so?"

"That's simple. You represent the spread of dairy-farming far and wide."

"Ridiculous!"

"So it may seem, from your limited perspective. Actually, it's quite important for society. Almost as much so as the deity whom you're destined to join."

"Deity? Will some god will take me in marriage?"

"Would you like that?"

"Humph. Not likely."

"It won't be so bad. But first, you yourself must become a goddess!"

Io tried to reply. There was so much more she meant to ask, but she could only bellow as the gadfly came awake again. It pursued her through dank Cimmeria and the harsh Chalybean midlands, out onto the meadows of the wide-eyed Amazons. By now the pain at her knocking heart had turned Io's whiteness to feverish pink; she blushed all over like a hot coal on the hearth. Rosily, she splashed across the Bosphorus, the "Cow's Ford," so named in her honor.

Zeus had forgotten her. Hera had lost track of her. The gadfly drowned in the Bosphorus, midway between Europe and Asia.

Still in cow form, Io wandered Anatolia of the lions. Instead of setting upon her, the lions roared to announce Io's coming and coughed politely when she departed again. Continuing southwestward, Io grazed by the Euphrates with human-headed, ringlet-bearded, and broad-winged bulls. They also respected her, and warmed her with their wings at night. Io's gleaming hide turned violet, then blue, and finally black. Her human voice came back. Singing to herself, she ambled southeastward. Plunging into the Bab-el-Mandeb strait at last, she struck out for the distant shore of Africa.

Toward sunset on the longest day of the year, a new creature stepped from the sea at Punt. She was comely, strong, and quick: a dark-skinned virgin with thick curly hair, slick slim thighs, and the softness of sand in her footfall. Small horns, like the new moon, adorned her smooth human brow.

Io was Isis now; an Egyptian goddess in her own right.

★ ★ ★

Disorganized though it always was, classical theology centered upon a single, often irresponsible but always dominant figure. Savage invaders brought him down from the north into Greece well over three thousand years ago. As "Zeus" or "Jupiter" (Latin: "Zeus-pater"), he reigned over most of the Mediterranean region for more than a millennium thereafter. Yet Zeus was always more passionate than regal. His legend carries the cool, swirling aroma of a summer thundershower. To adore him was natural, but to love him would have been eccentric; it wasn't done.

Zeus thrust enormous enemies into darkness; he made and saved the classical family of gods. Yet his human worshippers received no compassion from Zeus. Like Jehovah, Zeus put his chosen people through many a trial. Thus the legend of Io presents us with a callous Father-god, a cruel Queen of Heaven, a painfully obsessed Prometheus, and a tragically abused Princess, all four playing out their cross-purposes in somewhat comic-book style. Is there any way to justify such violent nonsense? Perhaps not, but there were extenuating circumstances, as follows:

Unlike the Egyptians, the Hellenes never developed hierarchical priesthoods. Their religious authorities were poetic performers, not bureaucrats. The proprietors of local shrines and oracles bowed to no central altar. "This is how we chant the old stories and dance out the old rituals in our neck of the woods," they said in effect. "If you care to listen and take part in our festivals, feel free. But if you prefer to propitiate lustful Zeus and jealous Hera elsewhere or even to invoke the crucified rebel Prometheus, that's fine."

By the way, Prometheus seems the most provocative figure in all Greek myth: a proto-scientist. Like Eve in the Bible, this Titan plucked the apple of the Tree of Knowledge and passed it on. Essentially, that was his crime.

Our word "science" derives from the Latin "scientia," meaning knowledge, and one might well protest on Eve's and Prometheus's behalf that it's no crime to know things. But when one begins to consciously organize knowledge and shape it into practical patterns, the psyche divides against itself. Instinct retreats, beaten back and driven underground by intellectual constructs or formulas which prove firm enough to be relied upon in the daily conduct of life.

Soon, religious obedience to custom also erodes. And when that happens the deities within may punish us by inflicting intense, subjective dis-ease. Or, finally, they may withdraw, leaving our souls drier than before. "A dry soul is best," said Heraclitus. Opinions differ.

Greek mythology is neither so hot as our animal passions nor so cold as our rational cogitations. It opens onto both, and deepens both. By turns pleasing and upsetting, it gives rise to many second thoughts, and thus inspires endless moral debate. Here I'll briefly quote four famous commentators, each of whom has helped to shape the discussion for our time.

"To make the elements of a nature-religion human is inevitably to make them vicious." So Gilbert Murray suggested in his *Five Stages of Greek Religion*. "Once you worship an imaginary, quasi-human being who throws the lightning, you are in a dilemma. Either you have to admit that you are worshipping and flattering a being with no moral sense, because he happens to be dangerous, or else you have to invent reasons for his wrath. . . . The god, if personal, becomes capricious and cruel."

True. And yet, as H.J. Rose observed (in *A Handbook of Greek Mythology*): "Not even the grimmest phantoms of pagan imagination are wantonly malignant. They may punish the guilty, or pursue their own revenges relentlessly, or go to great lengths to vindicate their dignity, but they never do evil for evil's sake."

Edith Hamilton warmly agreed. "The miracle of Greek mythology," she wrote, was "a humanized world, men freed from the paralyzing fear of an omnipotent unknown. The terrifying incomprehensibilities which were worshipped elsewhere, and the fearsome spirits with which the earth, air and sea swarmed, were banned from Greece. . . . It may seem odd to say that the men who made the myths disliked the irrational and had a love for facts; but it is true, no matter how wildly fantastic some of the stories are."

That's a brave picture, not altogether in line with actuality. In his essay entitled *Hellenism and Barbarism,* George Santayana made a more cogent case:

> The eternal conflict between Hellas and Babylon embodies the moral difference between art and adventure, between experience and presumption. . . . Not in its source, which is animal economy; not in its motive power, which is animal will; but in its steadiness and scope, in its self-knowledge. Barbaric poets may now sing war and now the chase, now love or a mystic philosophy; but the Hellenic sage will survey and define the actual conditions of human nature.

Getting back to Io now, it's true her myth appears especially dismal from the moral point of view. On the other hand, it's always been especially dear to artists and poets. The legend of a girl metamorphosed into a cow, and then a goddess, is provocative, painful, mysterious, and ugly in part, like human life itself. Call her an innocent child, a tormented animal, or a nurturing moon-deity; Io was in fact all three—and more besides. That's how it is with human beings.

A Dolphin's Death:
A Creed Outworn

All down the ages, it seems, dolphins have made friends with people. Why? Is it for the sake of something child-like, unformed, in our natures? Is there some residue of innocence that clings to our species, something which dolphins recognize better than we do ourselves? What sparks their unexpected, unearned sympathy for us?

During the reign of Caesar Augustus, a humble Neapolitan schoolboy made an alliance such as the emperor himself could never have negotiated. He was skipping stones from the bay shore, early one morning, when he noticed a dolphin lazing in the waves nearby. It seemed to be observing his lonely sport. On impulse, the boy waded out as far as he dared, and called. The dolphin disappeared. A moment later, it was nudging up against this knees, inquiringly.

The boy opened his satchel and took out the bread-roll that he was supposed to keep for lunch. As the dolphin's smiling beak parted the next wave, he popped the roll in, to the creature's evident delight. Thereupon it invited him, by signs, into deeper water. And although he could not swim, the boy obeyed, riding his new friend's back. They played together for a long while. The schoolhouse lay some distance off along the curving bay. The boy was going to be late, or so he thought. But, seeming to sense the problem at the back of the boy's mind, the dolphin ferried him across on time.

Pliny, who preserved the story, notes that their comradeship flourished for some years. Neapolitan sailors became accustomed to seeing the boy flash past on his dolphin—whether schoolward, or on some secret deep-water errand, or, most likely, in simple joy.

Upon reaching the age of fourteen, the boy fell ill. Exposure to the winter waves had congested his lungs. He developed pneumonia. Breathing was hard labor now; his fever steadily mounted. In his delirium, he believed that the whole earth had caught fire. Piteously, the boy kept calling for the dolphin to come and rescue him, to take him safely away from the cinder-hot shore.

Could his friend have heard? During the boy's final hours, the dolphin revisited the place where they had first met. But this time it leaped straight out of the sea onto the pebble beach! Wetly gleaming, it wriggled and flapped over the embankment to the shore road. A crowd gathered. Some people tried to push the desperate creature back to its own element, without success. Snapping, thrashing, the dolphin shook them off, and expired.

In cities under Roman rule, the pre-Olympian, fish-tailed deity known as Triton was often depicted writhing high and dry over the public squares. That in itself betrayed failure of nerve, not to mention taste, on the part of the old-fashioned faithful. Once upon a time, Triton had been a gigantic deity, ruling the deep ocean of the unknown. But now nobody believed in Triton, not really; his statues were just decoration, like Disneyland figures today.

The Olympian deities themselves no longer dominated public consciousness as they had done for centuries past. Zeus, Hera, Apollo, Dionysus, and Demeter could be scorned with perfect impunity, whereas nobody got away with impertinence to the "Living God" worshipped as Caesar. Drought, disease, flood, famine, or warfare might still destroy a city here and there, but great Caesar could build them up again. Yes, at a whim.

Meanwhile, the Age of Pisces—of the Fish—had begun. Jesus had called the first of his disciples ashore from the Sea of Galilee, to be "Fishers of Men." Beneath the purple-beaked and helmet-beaded triremes of imperial pomp, a seemingly humble, totally unexpected spiritual groundswell was beginning to form.

Christianity proclaimed unremitting, eternal war between Good and Evil, God and Satan. Previously, the Greeks and Romans had recognized no such absolutes. Their supernatural protagonists had encapsulated the virtues and vices of human beings, thoroughly homogenized. Small wonder that the Early Christian Fathers, like the Hebrew Prophets before them, passionately condemned polytheistic religion in general. And it was true, as Christians never tired of pointing out, that a painful spiritual confusion reigned. Hence, when Christianity won out at last, thousands of local performer-priests and long-revered oracles fled in disgrace.

Yet the myths which the rising bishops reviled survived around the hunters' campfire and the farmers' hearth, among folks close to nature. The derogatory Christian term for such people was "pagan"—meaning "of the countryside, not of the True Church." Pagans instinctively rejected the monolithic Christian Trinity, wherein three dominant male or sexless beings—Father, Son, and Holy Ghost—coexist. Instead, they recognized an interlocking trinity of types: animal, human, divine. Their legends continued to celebrate what seemed a never-ending intercourse between those three classes of being.

Most historians now agree that the witches, warlocks, heretical sectarians, and wandering troubadors of medieval times were hidden aspects of a great underground river, the pagan subculture. This resurfaced in the Renaissance, ending Europe's medieval phase. Then it was that classical myth-givers achieved public recognition once again.

Every age thinks it knows a lot, and has forgotten even more. From Saint Augustine's day forward, throughout Europe, command of Latin was a necessary adjunct to civilized discourse. With the coming of the Renaissance, many a learned person acquired Greek as well. And thereafter, right down, through the nineteenth century, cultivated Europeans and Americans had the classic myth-sources at their fingertips. Wistfully, William Wordsworth wrote:

> Great God! I'd rather be
> A Pagan suckled in a creed outworn;
> So might I, standing on this pleasant lea,

> Have glimpses that would make me less forlorn;
> Have sight of Proteus rising from the sea;
> Or hear old Triton blow his wreathed horn.

—and everyone understood what the poet meant. From the pagan viewpoint however, Wordsworth's nostalgic lines would be regarded as unconsciously impious. Triton's horn is not something to overhear lightly, or for solace alone. Percy Bysshe Shelley had a keener sense of it:

> The breath whose might I have invoked in song
> Descends on me; my spirit's bark is driven
> Far from the shore, far from the trembling throng
> Whose sails were never to the tempest given;
> The massy earth, the sphered skies are riven!
> I am borne darkly, fearfully, afar.

Eventually, however, quizzical scholars and kindly censors sucked paganism dry of its ancient lies, poisons, mysteries, seductions, wonders, and glories—indeed, of its whole rushing life. The bubbling, sexually charged and tragically sustained substratum of pagan sensibility sank from sight.

The Wet-Lipped Deity

The moon shone on the slippery path. The daisies foamed about Semele's knees. The frogs croaked coldly as the princess penetrated the sacred precinct and approached Hera's temple. A huge personage, robed in blue, like a snowbank folded in shadow, occupied the temple steps. She sat with her back against the portico. The peacock shimmer of her hair, the knowing sorrow in her eyes, and most of all her quietude, invited confidence.

Like a puppy to its mistress, Semele ran. Like a girl home from school, she clambered up to sit in Hera's lap. Softly, the Mother-goddess stroked Semele's hair. "You're a dear child," she murmured in a voice like enveloping velvet. "Still very young and innocent, not sixteen yet. I've called you here because tomorrow you must marry the lord of Orchomenus. Royal wedding rites fall within my divine responsibility. I've come to help you prepare."

"Goddess, I'm scared to death. What shall I do?"

"Make up your mind to please your lord, my dear. He'll be in command, or think he is, during the first few years at least. Meanwhile, you may well learn that sex is fun."

"Fun, goddess?"

Hera nodded. "Not just for the husband, but for the wife as well. Not that it ever compensates for what women go through."

"But, what's going to happen when the lord of Orchomenos discovers—as he must—that I'm no virgin!"

Angrily, Hera stiffened. "Has some local fellow been fooling around with you?"

"Not an ordinary man. My lover always comes in animal disguise. He's been a ram, a swan, even a serpent in my arms."

"You're much too delicate," the goddess smiled, "for such masquerades. Bodily changes will sometimes addle an adolescent's mind. You've been having nightmares, that's all."

"I don't think so. Goddess, I've missed my period—three times already."

"Oh!"

"Are you cross with me?"

"Will you be meeting your lover tonight?"

"Yes, in the grove sacred to Zeus, before moonset. This time, he promised, he'll come in human form."

"I see. Now, Semele, listen. I want you to make the god especially happy."

"I will!"

"He may appear forgetful, even cruel. If so, don't let that bother you. Pretend that everything he says and does delights you through and through."

"I won't need to pretend."

"Quiet! Now here's what you must do . . ."

Nodding happily, Semele sank down through Hera's warm lap to the chill temple steps. Her favorite goddess had vanished, leaving clear instructions, however. That very night, without a doubt, Semele would witness her lover-god's full glory! Rising, thrilled through and through, she made her way up the hill to their rendezvous.

The princess called him "you," and "friend"—vague words but sweet in her mouth, and no less personal than the obedient thumping of her heart. "I'm not afraid," she assured him.

"I should think not!" said the young man whose form the god had assumed. He drew her down beside him. In the moon-dappled shade under the towering oak trees, they lay at ease.

"It's my birthnight," the man remarked.

"Tell about when you were little."

"Well, I recall a cave, and three wild warriors with streaming hair. They took turns dancing, dancing around my cradle, clashing their shields to drown my infant cries."

"Did your mother nurse you?"

"No. Mother I never knew. A black sow suckled me, and a wolf bitch as well. When I was weaned, the bees made honey for me, and wild doves brought berries from the woods."

"Where was all this?"

"In Crete, on Mount Ida. It wasn't long before my father came looking for me. His beard was mushroom-colored, his eyes were pale as dew, and he carried a rusty sickle. Naturally I ran away."

"But, weren't you just a helpless baby?"

"Never quite helpless. Amaltheia took me in."

"Amaltheia? Who was she?"

"Pan's mother! She taught me to drink from a horn. When I spilled, she used to stamp her cloven hoof so daintily. And every time the north wind blew, she'd take me up onto her fleecy lap. Hiding my face between her breasts, I'd listen to the music of her heart. Oh, my dear, it seems a thousand years ago. . . ."

"I'm here," the princess murmured shyly, adding: "I will comfort you."

For a while, joy latticed the shadows. And then Semele said between her teeth: "Grant me one wish."

"Yes, by the Styx, by the all-compelling river of death, I shall!"

"Show your full glory, here and now!"

Bursting bright with rage, the god surged up through the oak branches to the top of the grove. Like a rabbit borne aloft by a hawk, Semele hung gasping in his grip. Flaming, thunderous, he spoke:

"Did Hera—?"

As she tried to reply, Semele's tongue shriveled and fell backward down her throat. For sign-language, she lifted up her hands. Her fingers, fluent in love's caress, burned like votive candles before the face of Zeus. Her soft limbs turned to wavering smoke. Her torso shattered, showering live embers far and wide.

Cooling, sadly sinking, slowly shrinking back down through the treetops, Zeus returned to the secret bower where, minutes before, he had known ecstasy with Semele. Stooping, shamed, he caressed the hallowed ground.

Fiery bits kept drifting earthward through the branches overhead. Now something larger, shaped like a pear, wetly brushed the god's thigh as it fell. Zeus stood astride the object, listening. From deep inside the warm gold came a faint clashing sound. Was it swords, or winecups?

Thus did you announce yourself. You, twice-born son of Zeus and Semele! We drink to your dear mother! Also, to the Father-god. We celebrate your conception, in all its terror. As for what followed, on that point we remain reverently silent. Not to be revealed is the mystery of your double birth, Dionysus.

Accept our prayers. Come, curly-headed reveler! Help us to lift the heavy, forgetful cup.

The dreadful myth of Semele's immolation had a happy ending. Dionysus, the god of drunkenness, orgy, tragic drama, and dithyrambic music, was born from Semele's miraculously reconstituted womb.

A vast, impersonal, abstract pattern stands behind this legend. To see it only need one transpose the four protagonists as follows. Hera becomes an impartial, giving and destroying, personification of nature at its most hidden. Zeus becomes the burning, life-giving, ultimately devastating force of the sun. Semele becomes her radiant, ever-crumbling yet continually recrudescent namesake: the moon—which passes from the condition of a fingernail-pairing to full, silver-bellied pregnancy, and back again, monthly. Dionysus is their "twice-born son," conceived in the caved moon, yet springing from the secret places of the earth: vegetation.

The quasi-historical aspects of the myth are also compelling. To get a sense of them requires a different set of transpositions. Hera remains the same, but Zeus now represents the iron-weaponed, male-dominated Dorian conquerors of Bronze Age Greece. Semele stands for the subtle but victimized, female-dominated, old culture of the region. Their offspring, Dionysus, brings the vine, the grape, the maddening yet at the same time civilizing power of wine. Although wine must at first have seemed of small significance, it proved to be a crucial ingredient for classical culture.

Dionysus is thought to have conquered roughly the same territories that would eventually fall to Alexander the Great. Not only Greece, in other words, but also Egypt and much of North Africa, plus southwest Asia as far as the river Indus. That legend may well reflect the actual spread of viniculture and wine-drinking over what had previously been a relatively boring, beer-soaked portion of the globe, during the eighth and seventh centuries B.C. They say that Dionysus' favorite method of conquest was to drive kings crazy, while inciting their wives and daughters to sexual riot.

One thing certain is that towards the end of the seventh century B.C., and increasingly during the next two hundred years, Dionysus did win official sanction in Greece. The so-called "tyrants" (really benevolent dictators) of her chief city-states rushed to institute festivals in the god's honor. Among the leaders in that effort were Periander of Corinth, Cleisthenes of Sicyon, and Peisistratus of Athens (who also ordered up the first definitive editions of Homer). Thus, by the close of the fifth century B.C., Dionysus had elbowed the conservative goddess Hestia away from her place at the table of the "Twelve Olympians." He himself was now revered as the last and latest member of Zeus' family group.

Did he put his newfound powers to good use? The answer appears to be yes. This wet-lipped deity seems to have saved the Greeks from orthodoxy and given them a whole new lease on religious life! Looking back upon that miraculous phenomenon from his own crashing and burning corner of the space-time continuum, Friedrich Nietzsche saw it this way:

> It is a sure sign of the death of a religion when its mythic presuppositions become systematized, under the severely rational eyes of orthodox dogmatism, into a ready sum of historical events. Then people begin timidly defending the veracity of myth but at the same time resist its natural continuance; the feeling for myth withers and its place is taken by a religion claiming historical foundations. [But Paganism's] decaying myth was now seized by the newborn genius of Dionsysiac music, in whose hands it flowered once more, with new colors and a fragrance that aroused longing for the metaphysical world.

Not only the new music, but also Dionysiac orgies helped to revive Greek spirits. Then came a decades-long spate of sublime

drama, tragedies and comedies alike, performed at Athens' Theater of Dionysus as an integral feature of festivals honoring the
god. In Pericles' day, the democratic Athenian Assembly actually
voted to pay jury-duty fees to all attendees at those dramatic festivals. That's how important they seemed to the community.

As Aristotle was to explain, such incredibly gifted tragedians
as Aeschylus, Sophocles, and Euripides in particular, helped
"purge" the Athenian populace of its natural errors and insensitivi-
ties, thus preparing the municipality to make a fresh start following each year's festival. How could drama do all that? Aristotle
answered: by inducing heavy doses of pity and terror.

The curt classic tag "In vino veritas" makes no practical sense,
of course. People in their cups seldom let slip a lick of ordinary
truth. "In bourbon bathos and in gin deceit," would be more
like it. Yet alcoholic drink in general does sometimes facilitate
subjective implosions of apparently alien ideas. Hence, the recourse to alcohol or other drugs, which is commonly featured in
initiation rites around the world.

Modern life offers the same recourse, haphazardly. In the days
of one's youth, especially, alcohol or other drugs serve a sublimi-
nally initiatory function. Later on, one suffers secondary or de-
layed initiations in the form of "nervous breakdowns,"
"temporary psychoses," and so-called "mid-life crises." And on
such occasions, too, Dionysus has been known to descend.
Whether we invoke him, or revere him, or simply live in fear of
him, this deity is always dangerous.

> Whatever far-off world exists
> dearer to man than life itself
> darkness keeps it in her arms
> and shrouds it in a cloud.
>
> No one has found a way beyond
> What lies beneath is unrevealed
> Adrift upon a glittering stream,
> We sigh for some still nameless thing.

That's my rendering of a few key lines from *Hippolytus* by

Euripides. Surely, there is nothing unusual about our own inchoate longings. Everybody has them.

"The Greek audience, listening at a street corner to Herodotus reciting a part of his work, or sitting through . . . the Festival of Dionysus, were accepting as truth these interpretations of human destiny and the nature of the gods." So J. H. Plumb remarked (in *The Death of the Past*), adding that they sought:

> . . . the meaning of Time when related to themselves, with its harsh facts of birth, growth and death. And this, not curiosity, is man's first and primary involvement with the past, the deep emotional basis for his preoccupation with legend, with myth, with heroes, with gods, whether they all be monstrous or benign. It lies at the root of all preoccupations with the past—Chinese, Greek, Egyptian, Norse, Vedic and Judaic. And as might be expected, the answers that were given to the common man were as mysterious as the Oracles of Delphi, yet always charged with his fears and hopes.

Isn't this a bit patronizing on Plumb's part? The Athenian "common man" got far more history than mystery from Herodotus, and more frightening insight than uplift out of Euripedes. Besides, the citizens of Athens are known to have clustered around philosophers as well.

Among the latter, Democritus went so far as to insist that physically "nothing exists, except atoms and the void." Note that he regarded "the void" as an eternally existent entity in its own right; in other words, an element of "Being." Ready or not, Democritus said in effect, men and women must reckon with the inner and outer reality of nothingness. It's the mother of insubstantial dust, bred into our very bones.

We "common" men and women do yearn for something sacred to envelop our hearts and simultaneously illuminate reality. Yes, even if it scares us half to death. And on rare occasions, we may actually experience something of that sort. The gleam soon passes; was it an illusion? Who can say? The impermanence of our most vivid moments does not in itself imply that they were false.

The Bold Cosmologists

Fairly early in its career, classical Greek culture developed a crack. The crack widened as the centuries passed. It entered Western culture as a whole, and now it cuts across world civilization. I'm talking about the split between scientific thinking and more emotional or "poetic" approaches to reality.

Throughout the sixth century B.C., the cult of Dionysus grew enormously, celebrated with dithyrambic music, orgy, and tragic drama. But the same time-span also brought into being a succession of Ionian and Dorian double-domes whose findings anticipated modern scientific concerns. These so-called "pre-Socratic" philosophers set the stage for the climax and tragedy of fifth-century Athens, which Socrates educated against its will.

Thales of Miletus, who flourished around 585 B.C., was first to conceive the revolutionary notion that we don't have to invent deities in order to explain nature. The world was shaped by no god, Thales proclaimed.

In the beginning was water. Then land appeared out of the sea, through the operation of natural forces. What sort of forces? Well, something like the churning of the Nile River, which keeps on recreating the fertile farmlands at her delta. Matter is alive, Thales declared in effect, whereas the gods are not. Everything that we can see and touch originally arose from humble combinations and reactions of a chemical kind, in water.

The fact that Thales was mistaken doesn't matter. Somebody once joked that if Thales had championed the cause of treacle as the sole element, he would still be honored as the rightful father of speculative science. In other words, of scientific myth—which seeks to describe the invisible, internal causes and essences of things.

In the next generation after Thales, Anaximander extended scientific myth to include human origins. As Censorinus tells us:

> Anaximander of Miletus said that in the beginning a special kind of fish were generated by the warming of water and earth. Inside of those fish, human beings developed. They remained in the fish until they reached puberty. At that point men and women broke open their host fishes and stepped forth, able to fend for themselves upon the earth.

How's that for a compact evolutionary theory? It evokes distant echoes of Manu (the First Man in Hindu lore) whom the god Vishnu held safe in fish form. Also, the Navajo legend concerning Holy Boy and Big Fish.

Anaximander's pupil Anaximenes carried scientific myth further yet, into the realm of spirit. According to Aetius:

> Anaximenes declared that the original matter was air, for out of it all things come to be, and into it they are resolved again. 'Just as our soul', he says, 'which is air, holds us together, so air and breath surround the whole cosmos.' Anaximenes used the words 'air' and 'breath' interchangeably.

Such ideas are fanciful, yes. Nonetheless they may inspire. Making "air" synonymous with "breath" and identifying air/breath as the soul/matter which holds us together was a spectacular leap.

After Anaximenes came someone jolly, scoffing, and yet profound: the philosopher-poet Xenophanes. All is one, Xenophanes remarked, and this includes divinity. He noted that Ethiopians pictured their gods as being black and snub-nosed, whereas Thracians made theirs blue-eyed and red-haired. "If horses or lions had hands, or could fashion works of art as we do," he concluded, "then horses would depict gods shaped like horses, and lions like lions!"

Perhaps so. It's not hard to imagine a flame-crested Ares of the fighting cocks, a melodious Hermes of the mockingbirds, a lean

Artemis of the hunting hounds, a sleek, all-fathering Zeus of the bulls, and even a long-eared, split-lipped Aphrodite of the timid hares. How do birds and fishes carry out their far-flung migrations, unless led by deities in their own image? I render Xenophanes' most famous and frequently disputed lines as follows:

> We can vaguely discern
> the elements in churn.
> Certainty, however,
> find we never.
>
> And even if we were
> to show truth bare
> we couldn't know
> we had done so.

The next pre-Socratic philosopher to appear was perhaps the most enigmatic and compelling of them all. Our whole house is burning, Heraclitus said in effect: "Everything is in flux, and nothing is at rest." The energizing principle is pure fire. Poets lie. Homer should have been flogged for propagating rubbish. As for Hesiod: "He was supposed to be very wise, yet Hesiod could not tell night from day!" Could Heraclitus himself tell night from day? No, he confessed. He regarded all such distinctions as logically impossible. The reason being that:

> God is night/day, winter/summer, war/peace, satiety/hunger; and when incense is mingled with incense in the fire, people call it what they choose.

Last in line of the great pre-Socratics was Empedocles. He declared that, after all, life cannot be traced back to a single entity such as Thales' "Water," Anaximenes' "Air," or Heraclitus' "Fire." Instead, he proposed to show, "how, by the mixture of water, earth, air and sun, there came into being the shapes and colors of all mortal things, put together by Aphrodite."

Sicily, which had been colonized by the Greeks, was Empedocles' home ground. When death approached, the proud old man kicked off his golden sandals on the edge of Mount Aetna's crater—and disappeared. Had he jumped in, or had he been raised up to heaven? Empedocles apparently preferred to leave that vague.

Only during the tragic, romantic, lyric days of Greece at its greatest did many people of genius pursue abstract ideas with absolute, passionate enthusiasm, catch them, and clothe them in the most sensuous terms. Consider for instance this surviving fragment by Empedocles, on the eye:

> As when a man, thinking to go out through the wintry night, makes ready a light, a flame of blazing fire, putting round it a lantern to keep away all manner of winds; it divides the blasts of the rushing winds, but the light, the finer substance, passes through and shines on the threshold with unyielding beams; so at that time primeval fire, enclosed in membranes, gave birth to the round pupil in its delicate garments which are pierced through with wondrous channels. These keep out the water which surrounds the pupil, but let through the fire, the finer part.

If the prolonged pre-Socratic bloom of scientific myth was intellectually heroic and supremely imaginative, so was Socrates' own subsequent effort to direct the light of intellect upon human behavior. He bent our brains to ethical concerns. But the price paid for all this would be great. Namely, the inevitable decline of pagan myth.

Stand-off in the Agora

When Empedocles came over from his native Sicily on a visit to Athens and made his first appearance in the Agora, the bright young men crowded eagerly around him. The afternoon was sunny and hot, but the Acropolis—not yet crowned by the Parthenon—cast a cool shadow down across the stone bench where the sage chose to sit.

Doctor Hippocrates was anxious to inquire about the epidemic at Silenus, which Empedocles had halted. Anaxagoras planned to demand some solid data on the volcanic activity which kept shaking Mount Aetna. Protagoras wanted to know how things were going back in Thuri. And, as usual, Herodotus carried a whole list of questions rolled up in his fist. But somehow a ragged, chubby and ugly boy, no more than eleven years old, got in ahead of everyone. Tugging manfully at Empedocles' checkered cloak, he piped:

"Sir, what first inspired your poem 'On Nature'?"

The great man appeared pleased. His yellow teeth gleamed in the abundant black of his full beard. He beckoned the boy to sit with him. The others all stood, forming a respectful circle.

"Well?" said the boy.

Empedocles coughed. "Bronchial congestion," he remarked, glancing up at Doctor Hippocrates. Reaching out a strong browned hand, he touseled the boy's dirty hair.

"Listen, and I'll tell you. West of the large island where I live, there's a tiny islet which—to the untutored eye—seems nothing but a shipping hazard and a heap of slag. In fact, its core is crystal, shining night and day, veined with quicksilver and gold. That's the abode of the Crayfish Queen."

"You're teasing."

"No, for I've reclined with her upon the slick, all-mirroring floor of her secret bedchamber. Her twelve slim legs glistened, and they seemed like twenty-four. Her long antennae, delicate as eyelids, brushed my cheeks. 'Knowledge without enjoyment,' she told me, 'is like a skillet without a handle.' I took the hint."

"This is all very well—" the boy broke in.

"Patience, lad. As I was leaving the cavern of the Crayfish Queen, a strange notion popped into my head. 'Have I given you a child?' I said.

"'No,' she replied. 'Just the reverse.'

"I urged her to be serious.

"'Serious?' Her voice turned cold as the March wind pushing the rain under my door, and shrill as the alarm of my water-clock—which woke me up at that moment. I had a headache as well, a regular migraine. Now, the only way that I've found to relieve such headaches is by writing verse."

"Wait a minute," the boy protested. "Are you saying this whole thing was a dream?"

"Well, but it did inspire—"

"In that case, I'll repeat my question."

"Oh, no you won't! Run along now."

"You have been less than candid, sir."

"Git! And don't come back until you're old enough to appreciate the fact that dreams play straight into creative work."

The boy shrugged, and ran off.

Empedocles gazed after him: "By Aphrodite's delta, what a brat!"

Herodotus leaned forward in his cool, ingratiating way. "'Brat' is an understatement," he murmured.

"Interesting, all the same. Tell me about him."

"His Dad is Sophroniscus, a stonecutter up there on the Acropolis. The kid's a whiz at school, keeps telling the teachers to redefine their terms. His name is Socrates, and the betting is, he'll come to a bad end."

As Friedrich Nietzsche lamented (in *The Birth of Tragedy*), Socrates "stepped into a world whose least hem we should have counted it an honor to have touched. . . . Who was this man who dared to challenge the world of Hellenism embodied in Homer, Pindar, Aeschylus, Phidias, Pythia, and Dionysus? Who was this daemon daring to pour out the magic philtre in the dust?"

Because of his consuming passion for pagan poetry (an old Germanic lust, to which Goethe had previously succumbed), plus his dark suspicions concerning religion and science, Nietzsche failed to appreciate the pre-Socratic philosophers. Moreover, he despised the gains that Socrates' intensely moral and questioning attitude inspired. Nietzsche noted that such ancient Greek thinkers still "drive us." They're the charioteers, and we're the horses, he complained, with neigh-saying extravagance.

In *Thus Spake Zarathustra* Nietzsche wrote: "Beware of me, for I am a poet!" But so were Xenophanes and Empedocles, to name just two of the pre-Socratic philosophers. And of course Socrates himself, during his final days of life, attempted verse.

"It is an adequate description of science to say that it is 'thinking about the world in the Greek way.'" John Burnet made that famous remark in the preface to his *Early Greek Philosophy*. What if Burnet was right? It's true that modern physics passes far beyond the elegant simplicities of pre-Socratic philosophy. Also, that modern mathematics is in a class by itself. Yet, perhaps the thrust of these endeavors hasn't changed.

Erwin Schrödinger, the great quantum mechanics pioneer, had this to say (in *Nature and the Greeks*):

> Quantum theory, while extending atomism almost limitlessly, has at the same time plunged it into a crisis that is severer than most people are prepared to admit. On the whole the present crisis in modern basic science points to the necessity of revising its foundations down to the very early layers. This, then, is a further incentive for us to return once again to an assiduous study of Greek thought. There is not only the hope of unearthing obliterated wisdom, but also of discovering inveterate error at the source, where it is easier to recognize. By the serious attempt to put ourselves back into the intellectual situation of the ancient thinkers . . . we may regain from them their freedom of thought—albeit possibly

in order to use it, aided by our superior knowledge of the facts, for correcting early mistakes of theirs that may still be baffling us.

Perhaps our present passion for measurement and number-driven scientific speculation is overdone. It's nothing new, however. From Pythagoras through Euclid, Archimedes, Eratosthenes, Aristarchus of Samos, and Hipparchus of Nicea, the Greeks also elevated mathematical science to the skies. It seemed so "pure" and unchangeable, worthy of quasi-religious devotion. Besides, mathematics generally conformed to what could be observed—both on the ground and in the heavens.

Early in the third century B.C., Aristarchus calculated that the earth revolves around the sun. A century later, Hipparchus rejected that idea, yet offered many astoundingly accurate calculations of his own. Hipparchus, as Pliny tells us in a tone of shock, "presumed to schedule the stars for posterity!"

We go way beyond that. Scientists can now create computerized models of the cosmos. These display what appears to be a rapidly expanding but simultaneously reentrant star-bubble. It's sudsy, rather glovelike, roughly pancake-shaped, and riddled with black cheese-holes. This agreed-upon image is doubtless riddled with errors as well, which might account for certain inconsistencies. However, millions of Nobel-caliber man-hours have gone into it; the calculations involved can be computer-crunched until the cows come home.

We do need myth, simply to love and grow. And we have it. Not only in its primitive and pagan aspects, but also in sacred and scientific form. The poetry of scientific myth appears less evident to some people than it does to others. However, there it is. If the pre-Socratic philosophers and classical mathematicians deserve partial credit for this, it's also possible that they have led us astray.

The Lesson
of the Labyrinth

Standing alone before a vast, half-buried building in the dawn, a young man partly unrolled a ball of twine and attached one end of it to a stone doorpost. Holding the ball loosely in one hand, he slipped inside the building, down along a darkening corridor. There were no lights. The youth often stumbled on the downward-tilting pavement as he went. Bats flittered about him; their warning squeaks sounded like chalk on a blackboard. His feet and hands kept striking stone corners, sharp turns, and massive columns difficult to circumvent. Occasional low lintels bumped and scraped his head in the blackness. Undaunted he would retreat, threading the twine between his fingers and thumb, before blindly pushing forward in a new direction.

For over an hour, he carried on. Finally, in the distance a sugar-cube whiteness glimmered. It came and went. Now it looked like an archway. The dank air freshened. The mossy, snaking passageway became visible. Now he could see the flagstones of a broad misty courtyard. Taking a deep breath, the youth stepped lightly into daylight. Dropping what remained of the ball of twine, he peered quickly about.

A fat person, down on his hands and knees, was doing something to the grass between the stones. Eating it, in fact! And now he raised his heavy, horned bull-visage. He looked around.

"I am Theseus, prince of Athens," the young man announced. "I've come to destroy you."

"How brave!" the monster snorted, sitting back on his haunches. Hands to muzzle, he delicately picked his teeth.

Theseus laughed. "Yes, I am brave. Ask Periphetes with his bloodstained cudgel, or Sinis the pine-bender, or the wild sow of Crommyon, or Sciron of the Molurian rocks, or rib-crushing Cercyon, or cruel Procrustes. I killed them all. But you look relatively easy—a grass-eater!"

"What's wrong with being vegetarian? And why should you wish to destroy a helpless old fellow like me?"

"I must, to save the flower of Athenian youth."

"How odd! Let me introduce myself. My name's Asterion."

"In Athens we call you 'the Minotaur,' meaning 'the Bull of Minos.'"

"Well, that's not entirely inaccurate. As you can see, I'm a human being with the head of a bull. Minos, King of Crete, is my foster-father. Thanks to him, I reside here."

"Your king has conquered my native city. He exacts a heavy toll. Already, the lives of twenty-eight Athenian youths and maidens have been offered up in blood sacrifice—to you!"

"Ridiculous! I abhor bloodshed."

"Fourteen more young Athenians, counting myself, are due for death, in your honor, tomorrow!"

"Believe me—"

"Don't fret. Having cut your throat—which I am to do in a minute or two—I'll rally the hostages and steal a ship. We'll fight clear of Knossos yet. I defy King Minos!"

"My dear boy, I sympathize. But how can you ever escape the Labyrinth in which you find yourself?"

"Ariadne, your half-sister, taught me how to pass from your prison."

The Minotaur lowered his round red eyes. "She's misled you," he rumbled. "There is no way to thread this knot of stone. No, there is none."

"That's what you think."

"Daedalus himself, the wily artisan who wrought the whole thing, could find no means to pierce its mystery from within. Instead, he built wings for himself and his son. Launching themselves from this courtyard, they flew away—it seems like yesterday. But you have no wings, Theseus; nor have I."

Theseus pointed to the ball of twine. "Its far end is attached to the Labyrinth's door. Once our little business is done, I have only to pick up the thread again."

Stooping, Asterion sniffed at the thread. "Ariadne's brains have brought you, then," he said. "What will be her reward?"

"I've given my word that I will take her home to Athens and marry her there."

"I see. To exit—many are the ways. I told Daedalus he ought to tie a thread to one of the bats around here. Upon being blocked off from the courtyard, the bat would soon have led him to freedom. But Daedalus wished to escape Crete altogether. That's why he built wings instead."

Theseus drew his sword. "I thought you were a prisoner . . ."

"Self-imprisoned, yes."

"Why?"

"I got bored with Knossos. The capital is incredibly dull. Living there was like having whole years blotted from my life."

"You're telling me this place is livelier?"

"Oh, yes."

"You lie. You're here for one reason only. King Minos ordered your incarceration. You can't budge."

"Can't I? As a child of nature, I'm a law unto myself."

Theseus laughed a second time. "Where I come from, men make the laws."

"Think so, do you? All men serve nature, in their bumbling ways. Like sick wasps whining around a paper nest, they swarm the white breasts of the Mother Goddess."

"I disagree."

"Man is a fool. That's why he's broken, broken without fail."

"You're ranting now, Asterion. Broken by what?"

"Freedom, chiefly. Even the gods find freedom difficult."

"So you prefer imprisonment?"

"I'm free. My race is of heaven."

To the Minotaur's mounting irritation, his guest laughed a third time. "That's not what I've been hearing! Ariadne herself admits that her mother—Pasiphae the queen—became infatuated with an animal, a sacrificial bull!"

"Let's just say that Ariadne and I share the same dear mother."

"The moment you were born, the sight of you—monster that

you are—gave the queen's game away. That's why you're kept hidden out of sight, a shame and a disgrace to the royal family."

The Minotaur yawned. "Theseus, you've been badly taken in. It's your own fault for asking stupid questions. Young men of your sort would like to see the stars in the sky all explained."

"I am like that. 'Asterion' means 'Starry,' doesn't it? Would you care to tell me—before you die—how you came by that name?"

"The stars are grandchildren of the sun and moon, like me."

"What a pretentious comparison!"

"Of course. We Cretans are all liars anyhow."

A brief silence ensued, whereupon the misty archways all around the courtyard murmured, each in turn:

> "Listen
> Theseus."
>
> "Beware."
>
> "Asterion
> has more
> between
> his horns
> than you
> imagine."
>
> "These things
> are true!"

Theseus drew his sword. "I thought we were alone."

"Never!" the Minotaur bellowed, rolling his bloodshot eyes. "Never in the Labyrinth." And the voices chorused:

> "Not in the ear
> of this island.
>
> "Nor in the eye
> of the sea."

Fiercely, Theseus glanced around.

"My solitude," Asterion said, lowering his horns, "is a sort of dance floor." He stamped his foot. From under the flagstones, a loud groan arose.

Theseus shuddered. "What was that?"

Lightly stamping in time to his own words, the Minotaur seemed to murmur in a humming tone: "Under every stone has gone a human bone, one alone, for what your race has done."

"You'll never dance on my bones, Asterion! I fear nothing!"

"Fear nothing," the voices echoed mildly.

The Minotaur glanced up, then down again. Had he cast a spell just then? His coarse white eyelashes obscured the malevolent cochineal of the monster's eyes.

Theseus was running down the slope of a sunny meadow, trying to reach Ariadne, where she lay in imminent danger—or so he thought. Like snow upon the mountains of Lebanon, a sleek bull loomed above the lovelorn girl. The white light off him, and yellow from the buttercups, glazed Ariadne's delicate thighs. His huge rough testicles furrowed the turf. His crimson sex emerged, steaming, to nudge between her knees. . . . The vision faded as the Minotaur charged.

Returning to his senses, Theseus flung himself down flat beneath the sweeping horns. Clanging upon the pavement, his sword sprang from his grip.

Grunting, Asterion tumbled over him, rose with an easy motion, turned, and charged a second time.

Rising to his knees, Theseus regained his sword and met the charge head-on. Thrusting upward, he pierced between the swaying dewlaps of the monster's throat. The voices from the archways and beneath the flagstones cried out briefly, all at once, in agony.

Asterion's shaggy head snapped upright; Theseus' sword had severed his ventriloquist larynx. Now his sharp horns pointed harmlessly heavenward, his spine straightened, his heavily muscled arms and small, grass-stained hands dangled limp. The creature hovered on tiptoe, ice-cold with shock. Now he toppled over backward with the weapon stuck upright in his throat.

Theseus got up. Setting one foot upon Asterion, he gripped the sword, twisted it, and pulled the blade free of the wound.

Bull blood bubbled chuckling forth. It fountained up around him where he stood, bestarred in red.

The clash between Theseus and the Minotaur is for always. No one will ever reach the end of that legend. But one thing it represents for me is this: the eternal conflict between the analytical and creative aspects of human consciousness.

To begin with Theseus, he's aspiring, brave, willful, extroverted, sharp-edged, a figure of decision who never looks back. One might describe this hero as left-brained, cold and moist; there's something almost metallic about him. Theseus personifies science, if you will. Dense and yet keen, he gleams with liberating force.

Ariadne's thread, the center-term of the conflict, is a memory device which cancels out the forgetfulness aspect of the Labyrinth. And Ariadne herself personifies the passively courageous, endlessly resourceful, and lovingly restorative element in every psyche.

As for the Minotaur, he's private, content, introverted, solitary, half-asleep. Until his polar opposite steps lightly down onto his moon-paved home ground, the sleek beast-headed man sits at peace, inviolable. The Minotaur personifies the artist in each one of us. There's something dry, vain, loose, fiery, free and easy about this monster. He neither knows nor cares that in a certain sense the world turns and returns around his secret name: "Asterion."

We come upon such dream figures—compressed and changed beyond recognition, of course—rattling furiously about and stirring up flurries of neurons in our own mental labyrinths. There, too, Theseus and the Minotaur struggle for dominance. Whenever either one wins, we lose. That's because in order to achieve soul-balance or spiritual wholeness, we must give respectful credence to both sides of ourselves.

Shakespeare and Goethe balanced out their objective/analytical and subjective/creative aspects—holding both at arm's length, as it were. That goes for Isaac Newton, also. Einstein did the same.

Cleopatra:
The Long Way Home

M arc Antony lay dead. He lay in state, forever disgraced. Cleopatra's sovereign power seemed certain to follow Antony to the grave. Soon Rome would reign over Egypt. Darkness had fallen. In a tower room of her palace, Cleopatra quietly sat and talked. No lord or lady of the court would ever see her weep. The Nile-brown queen had made up her mind to that. She kept four slave girls by her; no one else. The first of the four was a jet-black Nubian. The second was a snub-nosed Pysillian. The third was Nabatean, typically olive-colored, with crinkly blue-black hair. The fourth and last of Cleopatra's favorite slaves was a pinkish white Cretan girl, blessed with a coinlike profile.

In the midst of their circle squatted a bronze satyr, whose round belly contained lamp-oil. A lighted wick protruded from the figure's erect, highly polished phallus. The oil flame flickered and flared alarmingly, shooting jagged shadows up around the walls. Although gloomy in the extreme, the scene had a feverish overtone. Being unobserved, Cleopatra and her favorite slaves made no special effort to conduct themselves with dignity. They could have been mistaken for a coven of witches huddling together.

A sewing basket lay by the Pysillian's knee. Among its spools and needles, a pet asp restlessly wound itself about. Lifting up its small triangular head, the viper licked the air as if to write something with its forked tongue. Then, slipping between the Pysillian's fingers, it slithered up onto Cleopatra's lap. Absently, with her long polished fingernails, the queen fondled the little creature. "He's so cool," she observed, "and smooth."

"Careful," the Pysillian warned. "He's not been milked." Reaching across, the Pysillian roughly grabbed the viper and shoved it headfirst into her basket. "I myself needn't worry," she explained. "My tribe's immune to snakebite."

"How odd," the Cretan slave remarked.

"Oh, yes? Your tribe also keeps serpent pets."

"We Greeks are not a tribe. Nor friends to vipers, if you please. Our 'pets,' as you call them, are not poisonous but powerful. They're golden in color, up to eleven feet long. Great mousers, too—better than cats. We worship them as household deities."

"You're talking about Greek peasantry," the queen said. "Sophisticated people may revere snakes in the abstract, but we don't actually worship individual serpents."

"Begging your pardon, ma'am! When our divine snakes lick our ears, we do hear voices from beyond the grave."

"Ah? Tell us, then, what those voices of yours go on about."

"Doom. You know. Nine times out of ten."

"That's so Greek!" Cleopatra laughed, cheerful for a brief moment. "Nine times out of ten: unmitigated doom. The tenth time, what do they announce?"

"A noble birth. The coming of someone supreme, like Alexander the Great. His true father, by the way, was Zeus in the form of a snake!"

"I hate snakes," the Nabatean slave put in. "Around Petra, where I was born, we have the flying kind—with small wings like a bat's. They'll flutter along, a few feet off the ground, for a hundred yards at time."

The queen nodded. "I've seen their skeletons, in drifts up to six inches deep, out on the Sinai desert."

"Yes, Majesty. Every spring, our flying snakes make a run at Egypt. But your black ibises descend upon Sinai to beat them back. It's birds against serpents. But why do the birds always win?"

"Egypt is holy, therefore inviolable," the queen explained. "My native animals are sacred, every one. That's why we bury them with honors. The ibises you mentioned are laid to rest at Hermopolis. Fieldmice and hawks are interred at Buto. Cats, we embalm at Bubastis. Pigs, we sacrifice at full-moon time, with flute-play-

ers in attendance. Cows have our special reverence. They're sacred
to the horned moon-goddess Isis, who was once a heifer herself.
When bulls die, we bury them with one or both horns sticking
up out of the ground. That draws in forces from the starry realm
to energize Egyptian earth. But why go on? My land is the
world's richest, in every sense."

Up to that point the Nubian slave had said nothing. Now she
asked: "What about your crocodiles, ma'am?"

"Those we lay to rest, each in a porphyry sarcophagus, by
Lake Moeris."

Opening her eyes as wide as she could, so that their whites
showed almost all the way around, the Nubian expressed as-
tonishment. "Whatever for?"

"It's a question of courtesy, my dear. We're touched by their
behavior. The creatures always smile, from the banks of the Nile,
as we glide by in our gilded barges."

"Well, we eat ours. In return, they kidnap our babies now
and then."

Cleopatra grimaced. "How rude, and how sad. Those are not
Egyptian animals."

"No ma'am, but they look the same. And if I may say so, they
seem more useful than yours. We grind up their grinning teeth
to make aphrodisiac powders. Plus, we sell their dung to Punt—
for face-cream manufacture."

"Oh!" Cleopatra was shocked. "I've used imported Punt cos-
metics all my life. Not only that, but my Lord Marc Antony
regularly dosed himself with Nubian aphrodisiacs. Were ground-
up crocodile teeth in those?"

"Undoubtedly, ma'am."

"This is terrible; let's change the subject."

"Let's talk about sex," the Cretan suggested. "Are men more
fun to sleep with than women?"

Everyone laughed, except the queen. A thoughtful silence followed.

"Well," said the Nabatean at last, "men make you pay in the
most painful way. By giving birth, I mean."

Cleopatra shrugged. "That I don't know about. Like my country, I too have spread myself to the invader, while remaining

secretly inviolable. My black ibisis beat down the flying serpents. My children were all three adopted; I held none at my breast. In the esoteric sense of the word, I'm virgin still."

The lamp-oil had mostly burned off; the flame of the satyr's phallus was guttering. With shears from her basket, the Pysillian trimmed the wick, to steady it. She failed to notice the asp, which slithered away a second time, winding himself up onto Cleopatra's lap again.

"So much is buried here!" The queen's voice was vibrant. Unconsciously, it may have been, her fingers closed upon the asp. With cruel suddenness, she clapped his gaping jaws to the cool nipple of her left breast. Painlessly, it appeared, those little hollow fangs—unmilked, as the Pysillian had warned—played their poison into the royal bloodstream.

Myth graces; history braces. But sometimes myth and history come blended together, like perfume in a drop of sweat. In peculiar cases such as Cleopatra's, would it be right to speak of history as myth? How about myth as history?

Among Cleopatra's titles was "Thea Neotera," the New Goddess. She must have played that role on certain ceremonial occasions, but the queen was also a brilliant sophisticate in a time of intellectual ferment. She must have been aware of Plato's ever-popular *Dialogues*. Also of Aristotle's long-ignored *Pragmateia,* which returned to fashion during her lifetime. However, those writings may have seemed a bit musty to her. The Golden Age which produced them had long since given way to the comparatively anxious and syncretic "Hellenistic" culture.

In Cleopatra's time, two conflicting philosophies pervaded the Roman Empire's aristocratic and professional classes. One was the reclusive hedonism advocated by Epicurus (342–268 B.C.). The other, still more influential, was Stoicism.

The Stoic school had been founded by Zeno at Athens about the year 310 B.C. Zeno held philosophic court in the shelter of the so-called "painted stoa," the portico overlooking the Athenian agora. His teachings harked back to what he regarded as the real Socrates, not the one whom Plato had immortalized. Zeno believed that Socrates had taught mainly by example, inculcating the supreme virtues of honesty, dignity, and courage in one's conduct of life.

"Don't whine," Zeno said in effect. "Don't fight your destiny but go with it in a large-hearted way." The epitome of courage, Socrates had invited his own death at last. "You can do the same if that seems appropriate," Zeno assured his followers. "It's certainly no shame."

There was another side as well to Zeno's teaching. He seems to have condemned slavery and eerily anticipated Christian doctrine. According to Plutarch, Zeno argued "that we should regard all men as fellow-parishioners and fellow-citizens. There ought to be one way of life and one system of order, as it were of one flock on a common pasture feeding all together under a common law."

Within the limits set by her royal and religious responsibilities, Cleopatra probably lived and died a Stoic. During the centuries to come, many a Christian martyr would do the same.

In his *Prologue to a History of Philosophy,* José Ortega y Gasset put the case for what he called "the historical sense" as follows:

> It is this organ that grants to man the farthest distance he can travel away from himself, while at the same time it presents him, on the rebound, with the clearest self-understanding possible. While trying to comprehend former generations he discovers the suppositions by which they lived, meaning their limitations. At the same time he realizes the implied conditions under which he himself exists, and the limitations circumscribing his own life. By taking the detour called history, he becomes aware of his own boundaries—and that's the only way to transcend them.

Ortega concluded his case in a burst of optimism. The historical sense, he decided, casts a whole new light on philosophy itself:

> What looked like a smothering mass of errors and clashing opinions—completely irrational—begins to appear instead as a well-ordered evolution, a continuity in which human thinking progresses rationally from one conception to another. The systems succeed one another intelligibly. An irreducible residue

of discrepancies between a fixed variety of viewpoints does remain, but this no longer has an arbitrary character. The impossibility of comprehending the whole universe from any single position justifies the existence of a variety of fundamental conceptions—which thus prove inevitable.

Ortega's formula applies to mythology also. Unless we take long detours through other people's myths, we'll never know where we ourselves stand, or why. But simply adding mythic treasure to one's personal store of knowledge does not in itself suffice. We must also imagine our way into myth, as best we can, like actors in a play. If we're not prepared to make that effort, how can we ever fulfill our own roles in the universal drama?

· PART THREE ·

The World Reborn

While reading aloud from the present manuscript one evening at a local cafe, I took advantage of the occasion to ask for comments. Many were helpful, but the observation I valued most was offered privately, after the reading, by an extremely earnest young stranger.

"God made everything, just the way he wants it," the man began. "That is reality. Now here you come with a basketful of fantasies and hang them up on a line, like some prostitute's lacy underwear, for all the world to ogle. This is sick. Think about it. You're assuming a grave responsibility!"

Warmly shaking the fellow's hand, I thanked him for having relieved my mind. "Just lately," I explained, "I've worried about getting soft. Intellectually, I mean. The syncretic pursuit is all well and good—inclusiveness does deepen the soul-mix—but what's my basic position with regard to religion, for example? You've helped me to clarify that. Not gravely but gladly do I assume responsibility! Responsibility for my conscience, yes, and also for my own imagination!"

"You're mad!" he said.

"—and I deplore passive acquiescence in what you call the Creator's will. I don't for one moment accept your tacit assumption that the divine is separate from ourselves and inimical to our creative endeavors. Take away the human mind, and where is 'reality' then? Imaginative participation in what you call reality is not a sin; it's a necessity of nature. On that point primitive, pagan, sacred and scientific myth, all four, agree."

In Part Three of the present book, as promised, I shall celebrate the sacred power of Imagination. We would all be as blind as bats in broad daylight, if we didn't have that.

The Epic Journey of Dineh

Long ago, a certain young Navajo strayed southeastward from his native hunting ground in search of magic. His name is secret, so here I shall call him "Dineh." His legend, like the stories of most heroes, begins badly. Hostile Utes captured him. They held Dineh in their council lodge, well-bound, while passing their ceremonial pipe around the circle and debating, each in turn, what to do with him.

Dineh could not understand their language, but he heard something else. Namely the "Hu! Hu! Hu!" of Talking God's approach. The Utes heard it not. Then white lightning came down through the smoke-hole and hovered over the Utes' heads, but they saw it not. Finally Talking God entered, stood upon the lightning, and addressed Dineh as follows:

"What is the matter with you, my grandchild? You take no thought about anything. You must help yourself or else, in the morning, you will be whipped to death. That's what the council has declared."

As Talking God vanished, a dove flew down through the smoke-hole. The Utes paid no attention to it either. After circling the tent four times, the dove flew out again. Meanwhile, the Utes all nodded off to sleep. Seizing this opportunity, Dineh quietly loosed his bonds and fled through the night.

At daybreak the Utes woke up. It wasn't long before they mounted a furious pursuit. Dineh used various tricks and acrobatic feats to escape them, but eventually exhaustion set in. At that point Talking God spoke to him again. "My grandchild, are you still here? Have you come only this far?"

"I'm here," Dineh mournfully replied. "Regard my torn and bleeding limbs! I'll struggle on for a final few yards, perhaps. Then I'll collapse."

"Go then. Climb the hillock which lies ahead. As you take the very last step to the top of the hillock, close your eyes tight!"

Dineh did as he was told. Then, planting both feet firmly on the top of the hillock, he opened his eyes again—to find himself on the bare summit of a lofty peak! The mountain at his feet was seamed with deep canyons and clothed with forests of pine and spruce. Beyond the rocky foothills far below, he could barely discern the dust of his baffled pursuers.

After a day and a night of contemplation, Dineh felt like a new man. Gratefully, he descended in the direction of home. Along the way, Dineh was invited to visit the sacred dwellings of the Bear, Serpent, Squirrel, Skunk and Porcupine people. He also penetrated the rock-crystal house of the Nameless Goddess. He was even able to converse with Lightning Birds and Butterfly Women. Further, he received nourishment at the empty house of Corn Pollen—with the daylight door. In the clear depths of the House of Dew, long-bodied goddesses cossetted him.

Finally, he came to a house of cherry trees, where four gods lived. Each of the four looked exactly like himself, and each had the same name as himself! These four divine selves showed him a dance in which they thrust arrows down their own throats and drew them safely out again. "Teach this dance to your people," they told him, adding: "The dancers must take good care not to break the arrows in swallowing them. We expect your return."

Safely rejoining his people at last, Dineh taught them all that he had learned. Then one day he went out hunting with his younger brother. Coming to a place called Dsilijin, where the Black Mountains look towards Totsil, they sat down to rest.

"Something good is going to happen," said Dineh. "What it is, I don't know." They were quiet together. And then, after a time Dineh exclaimed: "Behold the holy ones! They come for me. Younger Brother, farewell!" With that, he vanished, but his voice continued on for a moment or two, saying:

"In spring, when showers shimmer down and slow-rolling thunder sounds, remember Dineh! Again at harvest time, when grasshoppers shake and shrill their green shins to make an orchestra, don't forget Dineh!'"

Listening with all his might, the younger brother closed his eyes tight. When he opened them again, he found himself back in camp, alone and brotherless. But following three days of miserable mourning, and three more of happy remembrance, on the seventh day the youth stood up to teach the people a new song:

> "From deep within the dark clouds
> these wondrous thunder-peals
> again and yet again
> make beautiful
> the land.

> "From far down among the plants
> these grasshopper grace-notes
> again and yet again
> make beautiful
> the land."

This Navajo myth contains a multitude of such songs, and it requires many, many hours to recite in full. The whole story provides the thread for an elaborate healing ceremony, namely the "Mountain Chant," which is still performed on special occasions in midwinter. The chant is coupled with sand painting, dancing, clowning, mystery-plays and social celebrations during a period of nine days and nights. A century ago, the Smithsonian ethnologist Washington Matthews wrote:

> The purposes of the ceremony are various. Its ostensible reason for existence is to cure disease; but it is made the occasion for invoking unseen powers on behalf of the people at large. . . . The patient pays the expenses and probably, in addition to the favor and help of the gods, hopes to obtain social distinction for his liberality.

Matthews went on to describe a particular Mountain Chant which he witnessed at Keams Canyon in 1882. Early on the ninth night, he tells us, the crucial healing dance began. I'll paraphrase his description:

Aside from the small "orchestra" of singers and percussionists, there were but two performers. The parts of their bodies that were not painted black—legs and forearms—were daubed with white earth, and each dancer held a great plumed arrow aloft. Moving slowly, with ceremonial gestures in each direction, they proceeded twice around the fire—from east to west by way of the south, and back again to the east by way of the north.

While this was going on the patient (a man on this occasion) was brought into the circle and caused to sit down on a buffalo robe facing the orchestra. Ignoring him, the dancers flourished their arrows, which were richly fletched with eagle feathers and carried triangular stone heads. Each dancer grasped his arrow between thumb and forefinger, about eight inches from the tip. Each gave a coyote-like yelp as if to say: "Thus far will I swallow it!" Then each appeared to thrust the arrow slowly and painfully down his own throat as far as indicated. While the arrows still seemed stuck in their throats they danced to right and left with short, shuffling steps. Then they withdrew the arrows and held them up to view as before, with triumphant yelps. Sympathisers in the audience yelped in response.

The next thing to be done was to apply the arrows. One of the dancers advanced upon the patient and pressed the magic weapon to the soles of his feet, first with its point facing right and then with its point facing left. Then he did the same to the patient's knees, hands, abdomen, back, shoulders, brow, and lips, in that order, giving coyote-like yelps after each application. When the first dancer had done his work the second took his place and repeated the same performance exactly. That done, the sick man and the buffalo robe were removed. The bearers of the arrows danced once more around the fire and departed.

The great plumed arrow seems to be the most sacred implement of all, and the act in which it appears is the most revered rite of the night. Its origin is well accounted for in the Mountain Chant. Once we know how the arrow is constructed, the significance of the gods' injunction not to break it in mid-swallow seems obvious. In fact its feathered section is a hollow tube. Taking the stone arrowhead between his teeth, the dancer slowly telescopes the shaft up into the tube to create an illusion of swallowing its first eight inches down.

Then he simply extends the arrow to full length once more while appearing to cough the whole thing up again.

We need our beliefs, and yet experience is often disillusioning. Result: we're torn between faith and doubt. This proves uncomfortable, even painful. We yearn to return to childhood, when we took things "on faith," wholeheartedly. And since we can't do that, most of us practice some degree of self-deception. Moreover, we willingly submit to a few beguiling illusions which are connected with myth, art, and sacred ceremony. Is this illogical? Yes. Is it wrong? Not morally. The deceptions I'm talking about generally promote human welfare, not the reverse. Such things often prove nourishing, even healing, to our spirits.

But that's not strong enough. What we call self-deception in others often proves liberating in ourselves!

When making a "leap of faith" into the unknown, we obviously don't have our feet on the ground. But the ordinary ground of palpable reality and time-bound day-to-day existence is not all that firm anyhow. Familiar, down-to-earth assumptions are not necessarily so. The unexamined tenets of so-called commonsense may actually hold us captive, or even drive us crazy. After all, what do we know?

There lay Dineh, captive, in a torpor, while his enemies decided how to put him to death. Then came Talking God to rouse him. Was that an "illusion," or was it sheer inspiration? Again, at the point where he felt he could flee no further, Dineh shut his eyes and immediately attained a distant peak, far beyond his enemies' reach. And from that unlooked-for peak—that newly inclusive viewpoint—he was able to pass freely down through the spirit world to reach home again. No small matter!

If we must sometimes close our eyes to open them in the myth dimension, so be it.

Bellerophon's Brilliant Career

Winter had come. The dark fell early on the town of Abdera. As the merchants lit oil lamps, their familiar booths turned magical. Well wrapped against the chill, the late shoppers sloped in silhouette to gaze on fiery carpets, crucified tools, slippers ranked like soldiers, and gold-washed sheepskins. Children scurried between them, surreptitiously snatching handfuls of straw from the scattered packing crates.

Beneath an archway walled off from the wind, the children stuffed the straw around a broken wheelbarrow—stolen, too. The leader of the gang, a boy about eleven, came running with stolen fire: an ember in a fennel stalk.

The ember made the straw spit sparks. The wheelbarrow sagged, hissed, and soon blazed merrily. Grinning like pumpkins, the children squatted around it. There were six of them altogether: five boys and a little girl. Stretching out their hands, they watched the pink firelight stream between each grimy finger.

The blind beggar who made the archway his home had been listening all this time. Now the heat reached him. Groaning with delight, the ragged old man dragged himself up close amongst the children. "Give thanks," he rumbled, "to Hermes!"

"Why Hermes?" The gangleader's tone was welcoming.

"Why not, my friends? Isn't Hermes the god of thieves like you?"

"And of beggars like you."

"No, beggars have no deity."

"Children don't either," the little girl put in.

"Childhood is brief." The beggar sighed. "And all life is mortal."

"Mortal?"

"Subject to death!"

"You're old," the little girl objected. "What do you know? We may never die."

"I wonder! It would be good to die."

"You're lying." The gangleader smiled. "You have the best time of anyone around. You never work, not even stealing, and what's more you never seem to cry."

"That I can't do. I've got no tears to amuse the gods. I owe them nothing now, except perhaps these twisted legs of mine. Or these—" He touched the drooping lids of his eyesockets.

A cart creaked past, drawn by a swaybacked horse. Between the cartwheels a tiny dog trotted, glancing worriedly about. The wooden shutters of the market booths were closing now. A shooting star briefly scratched the obsidian sky.

"If you like," the beggar said, "I'll tell you my story."

The gangleader poked up the fire with a stick. "Why not? Everyone be quiet so our friend can talk."

"They used to call me Bellerophon," the beggar began. "That's short for a peculiar honorific; it means 'Killer of Bellerus.'"

"Was Bellerus a bad guy, then?"

"He was. However, custom called for me to leave town right away. I sought refuge with the king of Tiryns, whose wife fell in love with me. I never touched her, but my host grew jealous. He packed me off to his father-in-law, Iobates of Lycia, with a written message. Not knowing how to read, I couldn't tell what the message contained. When he read it, King Iobates smiled as if everything were fine. Then he commanded me to hunt down a triple-beast called 'Chimaera.'"

"'Triple-beast'? That sounds neat!" the gangleader exclaimed.

"She had a dragon's tail, a goat's body, and a lion's head. Her breath was her chief weapon: sheer fire. The few brave men who'd gone against her were all reduced to ashes in gaping armor. So I walked very softly up into the wilderness that Chimaera inhabited. Along the way I found a winged horse named Pegasus. We became friends."

"Was Pegasus beautiful?" the little girl wanted to know. "What color was he?"

"Dappled, cloud-colored. His full mane and tail flowed like moonlight. His wings were silver-purple, like the inside of a mussel shell. They glistened like the banked oars of a war galley, rowing the depths of air."

"Could you ride him?"

"With his permission, yes. Together we flew against Chimaera. I carried a lead ingot, intending to send it crashing down onto the monster's head. She saw us coming, watched the ingot drop—and snatched it in her flaming jaws! Sliding, molten, down her throat, my missile quenched the monster's fire for good and all. She'd been a wondrous creature, but destructive as hell.

"Having thanked Pegasus for his help, I cut out Chimaera's tongue and returned with it to Iobates' palace. To prove my victory, I tossed the tongue into the fire, where it failed to burn. The king seemed grateful, but he ordered me right out again, to beat back a Solymian invasion of his northern frontier—"

"Wait," the gangleader interrupted. "Our fire's going out. We'll throw a couple of crates on it. . . . There, that's better. Beggar, continue!"

"Slipping away into the wilderness, I called for Pegasus. Mounted upon my friend, I hovered over the Solymian invaders, showering rocks from above. They fled in terror back across the frontier. Then, as we neared home again, I noticed Iobates' bodyguard hiding in ambush. The king had sent his own men out to murder me! We passed high over the ambush and then Pegasus set me down. Furious, I approached the palace on foot."

"Brave move!" the gangleader observed. "Did the king see you coming?"

"Yes, and he panicked. He ordered all his womenfolk to line up in front of the palace gate, hike their skirts above their heads, bend over, and bar my way with their naked bottoms!"

"How rude!" the little girl exclaimed.

"'Rude' isn't half strong enough. It was savage, barbaric. Filled with fear at the weird sight, I ran away again.

"So you lost, after all."

"Hold on. The story isn't over yet. Iobates ordered his own daughter to chase after me and beg me to return! As chivalry required, I obeyed. That's when the king explained about the message he'd received from Tiryns. My former host had written that I was a criminal violator of women!"

"What's that mean?"

"Doesn't matter. The point is, I had proved the message wrong. Iobates apologized for everything. He offered me his own dear, swift-footed daughter in marriage, plus half his kingdom!"

"Like in a fairy story!" said the little girl.

"Yes, and if this were a fairy story, that would be the end of it. But I had to go and spoil everything by taking a last ride on my friend Pegasus. Apparently, the gods did not approve. Say, by the way, has anyone here ever seen a god?"

The children's small, thoughtful faces drank in the firelight. No one spoke. After a long moment the beggar went on:

"Oh, what a flight we made that day! Below us lay the blue Aegean, pinched into whitecaps. The sky above was darker blue, cloudless but for the usual storms that play about the snowy summit of Mount Olympus. The air got thinner as we rose nearer to our goal, the home of the gods themselves. Pegasus was panting now, foaming with effort. He never swerved to avoid the stormclouds. Instead we shot straight up through them. . . ."

"Don't stop now," the gangleader prompted.

"Stinging crosswinds splayed the plumes of Pegasus' wings. Numbly, I held on to his wildly whipping mane. My teeth were chattering. Pegasus whinnied, a brave and lonely sound. Thunder replied. Were we flying or falling? Impossible to tell. Cold chaos poured past us, barbed with sudden cliffs. Burning, blinding, a thunderbolt elbowed by. Was it from Zeus? As Pegasus fought clear, I smelled smoke and felt a glancing blow which whirled me backwards and away. Solitary, without my mount, I strolled the vast and pathless air down toward certain death."

"The gods preserved you!" piped the little girl.

"Do you think so? A thornbush in a crevice broke my fall. Scratched out my eyes as well. These legs shattered on impact.

But certain shepherds had watched me descend. They rescued what's left of me."

"You were in luck, anyhow."

Bellerophon made no reply. He sat gently smiling to himself, as blind men will. After some time, the little girl asked:

"Did Pegasus reach the home of the gods?"

"I wonder!"

Especially if they conceal their sufferings, inspired men and women often appear arrogant. That's not surprising since they're blindly driven beyond the common ken. When I say "blindly," I only mean that they're not led or pulled along by some interior vision; not at first, anyhow. In the beginning, they ride their own unruly energies to skies on the edge of the supernatural.

Surely Bellerophon was impious in the eyes of Zeus when he mounted Pegasus and dared the steep storm-passage to Olympus. He fell, yet triumphed in spirit. Blind as Homer, crippled like the artisan-god Hephaestus, he lived to tell of his exploits. Pegasus, the winged horse, has always been equated with artistic inspiration. Bellerophon himself stands for the artist as hero. He sacrifices everything while struggling toward a totally unknown goal.

"I am certain of nothing but the holiness of the heart's affections and the truth of imagination. What the imagination seizes as beauty must be truth." So wrote the poet John Keats, meaning myth/truth, of course.

Callisto: Mysteries of Art

The "old masters" of Renaissance Europe were once young riders, and they also dared Mount Olympus. Take Titian's "Rape of Europa" at Boston's Isabella Stewart Gardner Museum. There Zeus is a small-horned bull, bluish white as skimmed milk or a June thunderhead, mildly breasting the wine-dark wave. His round bull's eye rolls slyly rearward to observe the princess who has mounted him. To her, the whole thing seems a game.

Velázquez' "Hermes and Argo" (at the Prado, Madrid), also projects a playlike quality, but there the game is deadly. The messenger-god and the star-eyed guardian of Io are both depicted as magnificent human beings. One is falling asleep; the other is about to murder him. In cloudlike heifer-form, Io awaits the outcome.

Between 1860 and 1960, the world witnessed a second Renaissance of significant painting, but that's past history now. In the present cultural climate, Picasso's "Night Fishing at Antibes" flashes dollar signs. The depths of that blue-green hymn to Poseidon cannot be seen. The same goes for Matisse's humorous homage to Apollo: his very strictly musical "The Piano Lesson." Both pictures are at Manhattan's Museum of Modern Art. Stony-hearted connoisseurs take them for spiritually depthless decoration, but that's wrong. In all great art, myth is reborn.

With silver-hued heat-shimmers in the east, lightning flashes along the western horizon, rolling thunder to the north, and fragrant incense swirling up out of the south, the mythosphere beckons us on, flinging open rainbow portals, cloudy or clear as the case may be—gateless gates, one might say.

The symbiosis of art and myth dates back a long way. Consider the Cave of the Bulls at Altamira in the Basque region of northern Spain. Equally awesome is the buried bestiary at Lascaux cavern, across the border in the French Dordogne. Art reproductions don't even begin to convey the wonder and glory of either place. Visiting them at leisure in the days when that was still possible, I myself learned something which our ancestors long ago forgot. It's more or less agreed that "all men are brothers"—and sisters, too. The Cro-Magnon cave paintings demonstrate that wild animals also can be part of the family. Lascaux in particular demonstrates a range of feeling in animals such as civilized people attribute only to themselves.

But just how did the Cro-Magnons manage to portray the animal world with such delicate exactitude while at the same time endowing it with ghostly force of unnerving intensity? The answer, I believe, is that artists who adorned the caves truly "envisioned" their subjects. I'm saying that visions of animals actually appeared before them along the multiple-curved walls and ceilings of the caves. The effect of tallow-lamp illumination, which swept flickeringly across the limestone cracks, bumps, and hollows overhead was doubtless instrumental in this. One can easily imagine how such warm, living illumination would bring forth spontaneous silhouettes, as it were from another world.

The miracle will have happened in the course of shamanistic rites, no doubt. Specific "visions" will have been evoked by "suggestion" which the chanting of mythopoeic invocations precipitated. Also by the "contagious magic" of pictures already in place. I'm suggesting a division of labor between "soothsayers," who chanted the myths relevant to the ceremony, and attending artists or "seers." The artists' task was to preserve each vision as it came with swift, clean, reverential charcoal strokes of a firebrand, augmented by well-placed smears of colored earth pigment.

As we know for sure from their art, the Cro-Magnon Europeans of thirty thousand years back were fine-tuned to the animal world. At that time, an ice age was ending, game animals were flourishing, and humans were relatively few. For a hunting people, the situation was paradisial. Legends telling of a time when humans understood the speech of animals, and actually married animals or were born to animals, recall such bygone days.

We have a reminder close to home, for Navajo sand painting preserves a Stone Age art tradition in our land. And yet, unlike the cave pictures of old, sand painting seems the opposite of visionary. Highly circumscribed, ever-symbolic and abstract, it is done by permitting minuscule streams of colored pigments in sand-powder form to dribble out from under the thumb of one's loosely clenched fist. Using this technique, a Navajo medicine man can create a considerable carpet in a few hours, all designed to represent various deities arranged in a strictly prescribed pattern.

Hundreds of such carpet-patterns lie folded in the brains of a few medicine men, still ready for ceremonial recreation and use. No sooner is the sand painting completed than it begins to be destroyed in the course of a healing ritual. The medicine man's patient sits down among the gods on the sand-carpet. He or she will be rubbed with portions of the picture, and perhaps eat a bit of it. What remains after completion of the ritual is at once swept up and reverently dispersed.

The originals of such paintings were done on buckskin, they say. The Sky People allowed the Navajos to memorize each one as a sacred trust for healing purposes. The Sky People didn't want their earthly counterparts to quarrel over material things, so they whisked the original buckskins away. The Sky People did the same with their ritual paraphernalia: whiteshell and turquoise baskets, plus arrows of turquoise, redstone, and abalone. Present-day medicine men use wicker baskets and reed arrows. To each they tie a semiprecious stone, by way of indicating its divine inspiration.

The Sky People inhabit an overhead territory which topographically duplicates that of the Navajo Indians. They're on what seems a higher plane, but this doesn't keep them from having spiritual intercourse with the Ant, Spider, Snake, Buffalo, and other peoples of the earth.

Sand paintings are the opposite of permanent, yet paradoxically they live for they return. They are as melodies to the violinist, or perennials to a flower garden.

★ ★ ★

Classical painting introduced something never before seen. Namely, illustrative realism of a syncretic sort. It put convincing images together in such a manner as to suggest invisible ideals.

Consider, for example, two mural paintings in the round temple at Epidaurus, once an internationally famed health clinic. The paintings themselves are long gone of course, but luckily the Greek travel-writer Pausanius described them back in the third century B.C. The first mural represented Eros, god of love. But this Eros had cast aside his bow and cruel arrows; he sat playing a lyre! The second mural depicted Silenus, god of drunkenness, imbibing from a crystal goblet. Through the crystal, one could clearly discern a woman's smiling face! In both cases, the artist had created a subtly therapeutic work. The first showed the pangs of passion replaced by musical harmony. The second crystalized from obsessive fumes a fleeting vision of beauty.

Among the more legendary pagan painters was Zeuxis of Heraclaea (a Greek colony in Italy). Zeuxis is said to have known the Athenian tragedian Euripides, and to have died at Ionian Ephesus in 400 B.C. That puts him around and about the center of things during the tumultuous "Golden Age" of Greece. However, not one square inch from a picture by Zeuxis or any other painter of the classical period (aside from vase-painters) survives. We can only read their reviews.

Pliny tells us that Zeuxis painted fruits so convincing that birds flocked from the sky to peck at them! But Pliny also states that Apollodorus was the first to give painted figures "the appearance of reality. . . . Apollodorus opened the gates of art which Zeuxis entered." According to Hesychius also, it was Apollodorus who first "mimicked form through shading and color."

Zeuxis employed five different models for his painting of Helen of Troy, incorporating the particular beauties of each one in his picture. And Zeuxis' most famous painting also merged differing forms. It portrayed the centaur Cheiron with his family.

Centaurs resembled humans down to the groin. Below that point, they were blessed with the bodies and legs of horses. Such double-bodied beings were thought to have roamed the forests and pasturelands adjacent to Arcadian Olympia. But after the first Olympic Games were held there in 776 B.C., the slow encroachment of civilization did its fatal work. Centaurs were extremely long-lived, however, and perhaps a few survived in Zeuxis' day. Be that as it may, his depiction was so convincingly done as to restore belief in the existence of centaurs! Looted from Greece by the Roman Governor Sulla, Zeuxis' widely admired family portrait was lost in a shipwreck.

Quintilian was one who credited Zeuxis with having established painterly principles of light and shade. But Quintilian awarded the palm for subtle contouring to Zeuxis' contemporary rival: Parrhasios of Ephesus. It so happens that Parrhasios composed his own review for posterity, namely the epitaph inscribed on his tombstone. Parrhasios' self-praise from the grave ran as follows:

> They'll never believe me, but
> this hand of mine has set
> the limit at last.
>
> No mortal effort is without
> flaw, and yet I'll not
> be surpassed.

In fact, no age of art and no one style, let alone a single master, will ever prevail. As the centaur Cheiron would surely have reassured Zeuxis, the artist's foremost rival was guilty of hubris. Visionary, myth-shaping power belonged first of all to humble, anonymous "primitive" artists. Nothing beats Altimira or Lascaux on their own ground. Or Navajo sand paintings, either, for what they are. Nobody can set "the limit" of art, as Parrhasios presumed.

One might as well try and set limits to the sun and wind, or to the mythosphere itself. Here's a story where art and legend intersect:

A centaur mother lay on the grass in the shade of Cronus Mount, suckling a pair of twins. She held one of them cuddled at the breast. Her other child sprawled out lower down, ingesting mare's milk. Cheiron, the centaur father, stood guard over them, stamping his hooves from time to time, or idly swinging his cudgel. His long white beard was winestained and his face furrowed with ancient passions, but his eyes were kindly and clear.

An ordinary mortal named Zeuxis had set up his easel to portray the family group. His left hand flourished a boar's-bristle brush, his right hand balanced a palette, and a paint rag dangled from his belt. The artist appeared to be in a fury, lunging at the panel on his easel, crying out and backing off again, only to leap forward and slash about anew in his southpaw style, slapping on the sepia or slinging in viridian accents.

"I'm sure we look funny, Zeuxis." The mother centaur said, laughing. "But must you curse?"

"Hush!" Cheiron murmured to his wife. "The man's doing his best to capture us—"

"Capture?" she repeated. "What an odd idea!"

Unheeding, the artist labored on. Mellow sunlight bathed the scene. A crow flew overhead, cawing. In the distance, a rutting stag sounded its thick-tongued, inconsolable bellow. The centaur babies had fallen asleep. Abruptly, Zeuxis laid his brush and palette aside. "It's done!" he announced, standing up straight to ease his back. "Take a look." He turned the easel around.

The mother centaur blew him a kiss. "You've flattered us!" Taking the children in her arms, she trotted off amongst the trees. Cheiron meanwhile uncorked a jug of wine. "Let's celebrate!" he said, stretching out on the turf. Zeuxis sprawled at ease against the centaur's dappled flank. Contentedly they passed the jug back and forth.

"This used to be Callisto's favorite haunt," Cheiron remarked. "She was a fine hunter—a virgin priestess of Artemis. I adored the girl, but she would hardly look at me, not that I blame her. Young ladies of delicate breeding seldom relish being mounted by centaurs. But Callisto suffered something much worse. Zeus got after her one morning in the guise of a brown bear. Seizing her long hair between his teeth, and her body in a bear-hug—"

"Spare me the details, Cheiron. That's terrible!"

"I agree. The Father-god himself must have felt some remorse. In any case, he stayed away thereafter. Not even when Callisto's baby was born did Zeus return. She called the child 'Arcas,' mean-

ing bear, of course. For his sake, and Callisto's, I pretended to be
the boy's father. But it wasn't long before Hera learned who the
real father was."

"As wife to Zeus, she must have been displeased."

"You can say that again! Hera cold is just as terrible as Zeus
hot. And although he forgets things, she does not. When Hera
came down to confront Callisto, I was present. Harshly, she ac-
cused the poor girl of having seduced the Father-god!"

"Hardly fair."

"Callisto embraced Hera's knees and watered her feet with tears
as she tried to explain what really happened. Zeus had raped her,
she began, in the guise of a bear . . ."

"Go on, Cheiron. Why do you hesitate?"

"Even as she spoke, Callisto's fingers turned to curving claws.
Her lifted arms grew shaggy. Her soft lips lengthened into a black
snout. Her supplications thickened to an inarticulate growl. Dropping down onto all fours, she came swaying over to sniff at little
Arcas, who lay asleep in my arms. And then, bewildered, my
dear friend shambled swiftly off into the woods."

Frowning, Zeuxis took a long pull at the winejug. "Hera had
changed her into a bear?"

"Yes."

"I don't believe it. Immortals are a law unto themselves, it's
true. But no force under heaven can ever change one form of
mortal life into a different form!"

"That's what you think."

"I do. Mortal life in general has one precious quality which
compensates for its fleetingness. Namely, the permanence of its
forms. Those were all decided upon when the world was young.
They're firmly fixed, immovable, unchanging as the mountains
and the seas from age to age. I worship forms."

"Is that the artist's creed?"

"Mine, anyhow."

"Have it your way. The fact remains that Hera turned Callisto
into a bear. Remember, I was there. And now I found myself
alone with little Arcas, one who carried in his veins the immortal
elixir of Zeus. I raised the boy well, here in these woods. When
he reached the age of reason, I confidently sent him forth to seek

his fortune. He succeeded so well that the people crowned him king of this whole region! It's still called 'Arcadia,' in his honor."

"Did you keep in touch?"

"Naturally. Arcas formed a habit of coming out this way on holiday. He did a lot of hunting around here. Hundreds of animals fell to his spear. But one old she-bear kept escaping Arcas. She showed a forest-shrewdness to match his own."

"His mother?"

"Don't rush me."

"She could have been. Did you warn him?"

"He wouldn't have believed my story. It's incredible, as you said yourself."

"Go on about the bear."

"One March morning, his hounds cornered the beast against a cataract. She stood up gaunt and groggy from her winter's sleep, regarding Arcas with a puzzled air. The falls roared at her back, making conversation impossible. The hounds yipped and whined with excitement. They kept their distance, however, afraid to close with her. The bear may have been growling; we couldn't hear. She was slavering, certainly, as beasts will. At the same time, she held her head tilted to one side, as if she were trying to think something through. She kept her soft ears cocked in Arcas' direction, and now her brownish-red eyes seemed to be watering."

"What did you do, Cheiron?"

"What could anyone do? The bear ignored me, just as she ignored the hounds. Her round wet eyes were fixed upon Arcas alone. She stood erect, and here's the most surprising part. The bear began to wave her forepaws, sweeping them inward with a clawing gesture, as if to embrace the king!"

"How did he react?"

"Arcas stepped as close as he dared. He stretched out his left hand in the bear's direction. Cocking his right arm, he stood with his level spear balanced on his palm and pointing right at her. He seemed about to hurl the weapon between her open jaws. But now, stiffening with surprise, the bear emphatically shook her head! Her hackles bristled, and tears were running down her snout, as my dear foster-son took careful aim—"

"Please, not another word!"

Surprised, the centaur glanced at his friend. "Well, I know how you feel. To tell the truth, I myself couldn't bear to look. At the final moment, I turned and left the scene as fast as I could gallop. But later on, I learned that an apotheosis had occurred."

"Apotheosis?"

"Hera can be cruel, but she's also the nurturing Queen of Heaven. She watches over mothers and children with particular compassion. So now she caused Callisto to disappear!"

"Are you sure?"

Cheiron nodded. "Unharmed, the she-bear dissolved in the mist of the rushing cataract. And that very night a new constellation appeared in the northernmost quarter of heaven. It's known to many as 'the Big Dipper.' However, initiates in the Mysteries of Hera call that constellation 'the Great Bear.'"

"Are you suggesting that Callisto yet lives, and that she hibernates in the night sky?"

"Better yet, she returns—as a young girl again."

"I see."

Rising, Zeuxis stepped across to the easel. He blew a bit of thistledown from the still-wet surface of his picture. Then he stood back with a weary, half-distracted air.

"Are you pleased with it? Cheiron asked.

"Oh, my friend, what strange things happen in this world! Things that no family portrait can ever show!"

"The Unknown God"

According to Herodotus, certain Aegéan fishermen once found a golden tripod in their net. Various potentates from neighboring islands claimed the prize. In the interest of peace, the matter was finally brought before the Oracle at Delphi.

"Whoever is wisest," Apollo's priestess proclaimed, "to him the tripod belongs!"

Overawed, the contending potentates joined forces, traveled to Melitus, and presented the golden tripod to Thales the philosopher, who taught that Water is the Mother of all Things.

Disturbed by this gift from the sea, Thales passed it on to a second sage, who passed it to a third, who passed it to a fourth, and so on. It was as if the mere presence of the prize made each man doubt his own wisdom. So the golden tripod kept on circulating until, on the seventh pass, it reappeared at Thales's own door!

Thereupon he discreetly gave it to Delphi, honoring the god Apollo as being wiser than any human.

Six centuries later, when Saint Paul appeared at Athens, the city had fallen under Roman sway. It was something of a university town, replete with public buildings of the utmost splendor, and with statues of pagan deities everywhere. Paul, shocked, stood up in the marketplace to inveigh against the local "idolatry." Before long, Paul was summoned to the open-air Citizens Council atop the hill called Aereopagus. Acting as an informal grand jury,

129

the council called upon the stranger to explain his ideas. According to Saint Luke, Paul responded as follows:

> Men of Athens, I have seen for myself that you are scrupulous in religion. For as I strolled among your sacred monuments I came upon an altar inscribed: "To the Unknown God."
>
> Such is my God whom I proclaim to you. Without being aware of the fact, you already worship Him. Since He created the whole world along with everything that it contains, God has no need for shrines made by human hands. Nor is He in need of anything that human hands can perform. For after all it's He who gives us life, breath, and everything else besides! He created the entire human race from one and the same single stock, you understand, spread out across the earth. He decreed how long each nation would flourish, and what its boundaries would be. He did so for a reason. Namely that each nation separately should seek Him, feel its way toward Him, and find Him at last. At the same time, He's never far from us as individuals. As your own poets have written:
>
> > "In Him we live and move and have our being,
> > For we are His children."
>
> Since this is so, we have not the slightest excuse for supposing that He resembles gold, silver or marble statuary in any way. God overlooked such nonsense in the past; He pitied our ignorance. But now He has a new commandment for us. Repent! For soon the whole world will be judged in righteousness. Indeed, God has already appointed a Man to do the judging! To prove it, He himself recently raised that Man from the dead!

The Athenians, who "delighted in every new thing," had listened eagerly at first. The stranger's opening remarks were perfectly clear and logical. However his ringing peroration struck most of those present as being ridiculous, and many laughed aloud. But "Dionysius the Aeropagite" and "a woman called Damaris" were profoundly impressed. Since Dionysius and Damaris were very common names, it's as if Saint Luke were telling us that almost everybody found Paul's message hilarious—except for May and Fred.

Judged harmless, Paul was released on his own cognizance. Athens had shrugged him off. Yet even there, in the chill shadow of the academies, the holy apostle had managed to touch a pair of understanding hearts. Before carrying his mission on to Corinth, Paul gave private instructions to Dionysius and Damaris.

Years later, when Paul was preaching in Rome and preparing his own inevitable martyrdom, he received a letter from Corinth asking what matters most in life. "Faith, Hope, and Love," the apostle responded, "but the greatest of these is Love."

Wisdom, that fine old Athenian commodity, wasn't even in the running, you see. Yet the late-classical Athenians were more "scrupulous," as Saint Paul put it, than ourselves. Hadn't they raised an altar to "the Unknown God"? Can you imagine such an altar on the Mall at Washington, D.C.?

Perseus: The Perseverance of Poetry

O n the Aegean island of Seriphos stands a headland capped by a rounded hill. The high hillside was hollowed out a long, long time ago, in order to create an amphitheater facing the sea. Three thousand years and more must have passed since the morning when Perseus stood on trial in that amphitheater. The seated statues for which the place was famous have long since toppled and worn away. Except for occasional snow-colored outcroppings among the blood-red poppies of the rock, the marble benches themselves stand buried now. But nothing keeps us from imagining the ancient scene:

The day chosen for Perseus' ordeal was sunny, breezy, and brilliantly clear. Fat King Dectes lolled enthroned at the center of the amphitheater's front row, facing the solitary youth on the stage and the blue sea beyond. A ten-man bodyguard sat flanking the king. The curving tiers of marble benches above and behind him were occupied by the adult male citizenry of Seriphos, some seven hundred strong.

Perseus had come unarmed, dressed in a lilac cloak woven by his mother and carrying a large covered basket. He set the basket on the stones at his feet, combed back his curly hair with his fingers, and stood waiting.

"You're an unwelcome bastard, a lazy dreamer, and worse," King Dectes declared. "So when you disappeared last year, we were delighted. Now you've turned up again, with a wife—an Ionian princess, you tell us—plus an immense fortune in gems and gold. You're buying land on Seriphos, driving real estate prices dangerously high. How did you amass such a fortune? Specifically, what crimes did you commit in the process?"

"I never liked you either, sire. I despise your boorish attentions to my mother."

"Contempt of Court!"

"Yes, I feel that."

"It won't help your case, boy."

"Your own case is the hopeless one."

"Concerning your mother? We'll see. It's no secret that I greatly desire Danae's company. But your mother can't get you off this time! So I repeat, what crimes did you commit?"

Perseus took a deep breath and began:

"Some time ago, the gods put together an artificial woman named Pandora, whose loveliness was on a par with my mother's. They endowed Pandora with everything you might expect—except a human heart. Then they gave the creature to King Epimetheus of Macedonia, who fell in love with her. Well, it wasn't long before Pandora murdered Epimetheus, his children, and many others besides. When her crimes were discovered, she fled north to a river called the Danube. There, she joined a tribe of female warriors, superb archers, known as Amazons."

"We've heard of them," Dectes rumbled, "but not the rest."

"Pandora soon became their queen, but under a new name: 'Medusa.'"

"Well, that's a switch."

"Medusa's rich hair evolved a serpentine life of its own, and her wide blue eyes developed lethal intensity of expression. She now proposed to lead the Amazons southward against Greece. Our whole fatherland stood in danger."

"That's quite enough!" the king cried happily. "What you say is all rubbish anyhow. No one ever created, or will ever make, a creature that looks and acts like a human being but isn't. Besides, there's never been a woman on the earth to rival your dear mother Danae."

Bitterly, Perseus smiled. "Mother warned me that you'd try to cheat. Under the laws of Seriphos, you must hear me out."

"Well, I forgot. Go on with your idiotic tale. Then I'll make you eat it."

"The gods were unwilling to destroy their own creation. However, it had to be done. That's why Athene enlisted my services and loaned me three priceless treasures. First, Hermes' winged sandals, for flying through the air. Second, Hades' helmet of invisibility. Third, Athene loaned me her own shield, burnished mirror-bright. With such advantages, how could I lose? The glory of my victory belongs in part to Hermes, Hades, and Athene herself, yet I alone destroyed the monster!"

"This is too much!" the king broke in. "Are you claiming that you killed Medusa? How?"

"You wouldn't understand. On the way home I met my present bride—Princess Andromeda—whom I rescued from the jaws of an enormous sea-dragon. My wealth, which you find suspect, is in fact her royal dowry!"

Dectes licked his lips. "Had your say now?"

"Yes."

"Here's mine. You stand guilty of imposing on our credulity. For that, you'll be punished five-fold. First, your fortune falls to the state treasury. Second, your so-called bride, the pretender Andromeda, will be sold off-island into prostitution. Third, as for you, young man, we'll have you stripped and whipped where you stand! Fourth, I order your mother Danae brought to witness your humiliation."

"Tyrant!"

"Thank you, Perseus. Fifth, unless Danae gives in and marries me of her own free will at last, I'll have you hurled from the cliff at your back! That's how we deal with lying bastards, boy."

"I'm no liar. I have solid proof. Medusa's head is here in my basket."

"So? Show us."

"I'm afraid to."

"Ho, ho!" the king cried jovially. "I'll bet you are!" Having been an actor in his younger days, Dectes appreciated what he called court drama. He was enjoying himself now. "Are you afraid we'll die of fright, or what?"

"Something like that, yes."

"Hey, this is rich. Let's assume that the mere sight of the monster's head turns us to stone. In that case, we won't be in a position to whip you, let alone execute you. With the island's male citizenry out of the way, our land, our treasure, our women and our children will one and all belong to you! By Hades, boy, you'll inherit Seriphos! Think about it. Show us the head, so we can die laughing."

Perseus raised his eyes to the crowd. His voice was clear and strong as he called out: "Citizens of Seriphos! You've heard the king. He's brought me to judgement for his own profit, but also in the interest of public merriment. He takes me for a fool who's putting on a desperate, comic show. Do you feel that way, too? I'm standing here on exhibition, a solitary object of scorn, so look your fill. Then ask yourselves this one question: do you also wish see what's in my basket, or not?"

Without hesitation, the assembled citizens roared assent.

Perseus removed the basket lid. Turning his face aside, he reached down and in. Still looking away, he pulled out Medusa's head and held it up. Now everyone present except himself bore witness to her serpent-hair—and her wide-open eyes.

As King Dectes raised his hands, his fingers froze in midair, his leering red face turned white, and his breathing stopped. From head to foot the king was marble now, a monument. Statues by the hundred sat around and above him, tier upon curving tier. Dumbstruck, utterly silent, cold stone where men had been a moment before, they would never rise again.

Perseus covered his eyes with his free hand. He turned to face the sea. Counting his steps, twenty paces in all, he walked to the cliff edge and halted there. He could feel the updraft on his face, with the sea's salt fragrance in it. "Let the fish feed on this!" he cried, hurling Medusa's head as far out as he could. He didn't watch it fall, nor could he hear it strike the water far below. Turning around again, he addressed his audience of stone:

"Except for Mother, older people never seem to listen anymore. Why not? It's always best to hear the dreams of young men and women. It's wise to welcome the news that travelers bring home. Truth does far less harm than insular complacency. Why couldn't you accept the truth from me and save your lives? From now on, you must harken to the wordless wind."

* * *

Perseus was the patron saint of poets. He flew swiftly anywhere he liked, at will, thanks to imagination—Hermes' winged sandals. It may be that his most real and adventurous moves took place in the mind alone, when he wore Hades' helmet of invisibility. And Perseus carried a shield provided by the goddess of wisdom. Burnished to the point of accurate reflection, his buckler mirrored everything it faced, turning the fearsome spirits of the void harmlessly back upon themselves. The shield is not the man, however.

"The experience of poets is akin to that of seers and prophets, who offer many fine utterances without understanding a word of what they say!" When Socrates made that harsh remark, he was describing contemporaries of genius. For instance, the comic playwright Aristophanes, who had lampooned Socrates himself in *The Clouds*. I'll quote a key passage from B. B. Rogers' lilting translation:

SOCRATES

"Zeus indeed! There's no Zeus: don't you be so obtuse."
STREPSIADES
"No Zeus up aloft in the sky!
Then, you first must explain who it is sends the rain;
or I really must think you are wrong."
SOCRATES
"Well then, be it known, these [clouds] send it alone:
I can prove it by arguments strong.
Was there ever a shower seen to fall in an hour
when the sky was all cloudless and blue?
Yet on a fine day, when the clouds are away,
he might send one, according to you."
STREPSIADES
"Well, it must be confessed, that chimes in with the rest;
your words I am forced to believe.
Yet before, I had dreamed that the rain-water streamed
From Zeus and his chamber-pot seive."

The tragedian Euripides was also among Socrates' acquaintances. A shrewd doubter and courageous flouter, Euripides burned with terrible wisdom, prophecy, and paradox. Consider

his *Herakles Crazy,* for example. In a fit of insanity, Herakles
(Latin: "Hercules") destroys his own little children. Regaining his
senses, he learns what he has done. His friend Theseus tries to
console him with the remark that, after all, the gods themselves
do strange things in their own families. But Herakles scorns such
comfort. He arises from the dust. With blood-clotted fingers he
dashes the tears from his eyes, declaring:

> "The gods do not commit adultery,
> Nor chain each other up.
> Such tales never impressed me; never will.
> Nor can I think one god outroars the rest.
> If God exists at all, He's perfect
> And complete in every part. The poets lie!"

Was ever a poet more anti-poetic, more passionately philosophical? Scholars have argued that lines like these betray Socrates'
influence, and perhaps they do. Euripides ended his life in exile
from Athens. His final drama, the bitter fruit of his old age,
climaxes with a bacchic reveler bringing what she believes to be
the head of a lion cub onto the stage. Ecstatically she boasts of
how—in her god-given power and joy—she herself wrenched the
head, while it still lived, from its lion body. The audience sees,
as she does not, that in fact the head is human. She's torn it from
the neck of her own beloved son.

Socrates had no objection to such shattering moments of drama.
What stuck in his craw was that none of his incredibly gifted
dramatist friends seemed able to explain or moralize about their
own largely intuitive labors.

> The poet plants something vicious in everybody. He pre-
> sents you with phantoms far removed from reality. He appeals
> to that part of you which can't even distinguish big from
> little. . . . So long as poetry be given freedom of the streets,
> be sure that pleasure and pain are going to rule your city,
> instead of law. . . . If the Muse objects that we are harsh and
> rude to banish her, let us reply that after all there is an ancient
> strife between philosophy and poetry.

Thus Plato, who was Socrates' most brilliant disciple, argued in *The Republic.* Plato deployed the historic figure of his mentor as a mouthpiece for his own ideas, thus giving rise to controversies which continue to the present day. But, strife or no strife, Plato himself sometimes used myth to make his points. In *The Symposium* for example, he attributed the following legend to a playwright named Agathon:

> People used to be eight-limbed and double-headed, male and female in one, joined back to back—or so the story went. These proud and happy hermaphrodites were so sure of themselves that one fine day they dared to cartwheel up Mount Olympus and storm heaven's gates! But Zeus promptly rolled them down again. And then, by way of punishment, he ordered Hephaestus to split each human in half! Thus it is that our severed halves so passionately seek each other out. Making love is a feckless effort to recover our former whole and high estate.

Plato told that tale to introduce a moral. Love is like a ladder, he supposed, with sex for a slippery bottom rung and sensuous pleasure above that. Next comes non-touching affection (so-called "Platonic love") between friends. Higher yet on Plato's ladder we find reverence for what he regarded as the right ideas and institutions. All this leads in time to the top rung—namely, Contemplation: "To gaze on beauty's very self."

Such abstract philosophizing drives true poets around the bend, up the wall, and over the top. It's just the sort of preachment that led the American gynecologist and poet William Carlos Williams to swear his famous vow: "No thought but in things!"

Plato would probably have puked at Williams' seeming materialism. He argued that all poets, including the classics, should be subjected to strict state-censorship and reinterpretation by the philosophical upper crust! And, strange though it may seem to us, Plato's recommendation was carried out in force. Throughout the rise and fall of the Roman Empire, the Byzantine era, the medieval darkness of Western Europe, and finally the cloudburst brilliance of the Renaissance, high-minded folk felt free to discover elevating Neo-Platonic, Gnostic and/or Christian messages in pagan myth. This recondite reinterpretation of the classics had the unlooked-for result of keeping them alive and well for many, many centuries. Instead of banishing pagan poets, the neo-Platonists inadvertently honored their efforts. Thus Homer and Ovid in particular were placed on the same level of intuitive genius as the Hebrew Prophets, and as carefully preserved. But finally some commonsense protest emerged. At the start of the Northern Renaissance, in the Prologue to his *Gargantua*, Rabelais had this to say:

> Do you honestly believe that Homer, when he wrote *The Iliad* and *The Odyssey*, had in mind the allegories which have been foisted upon him by Plutarch, Heraclides, Ponticus, Eustathius, and Phornutus, and which Politian has purloined from them? If you do believe this, you are far indeed from my opinion, which is that Homer could no more have dreamed of anything of the sort than Ovid, in his *Metamorphoses*, could have been thinking of the Holy Sacraments.

Martin Luther excoriated the "moralizers" of Ovid, "who turn Apollo into Christ, and Daphne into the Virgin Mary." Luther found his own analogy for such baroque allegorizing. He compared it to a robot-courtesan, a latter-day Pandora. Fleshed out by Beelzebub and seductively swathed in swirling incense, she's escorted by soot-feathered flocks of lascivious ecclesiastics.

Such cold blasts failed to stem the growing tide of what might be described as religious deconstructivism. Erasmus—ever the mediator—mildly suggested that it was better to allegorize pagan myth than to take the Old Testament literally. And the red-headed Canon of Gotha, Conrad Mudt ("Conradius Mutianus Rufus") penned a private letter asserting:

> There is but one god and one goddess, but many are their powers and names: Jupiter, Sol, Apollo, Moses, Christus, Luna, Ceres, Prosepina, Tellus, and Maria. . . . Have a care in speaking of these things. They should be hidden in silence, like the Eleusinian mysteries. Sacred matters should always be wrapped in mystery and enigma.

At Florence in 1463, Marsilio Ficino completed his Latin translation of an old Greek manuscript which had been entrusted to him by Cosimo de' Medici. The *Corpus Hermeticum* is a mystical text, not easily placed. It apparently harks back to Alexandria, the Egyptian capital founded by Alexander the Great, which became a haven of Hellenistic culture under Imperial Roman rule. Here's a key passage:

> [Man] is placed happily in a middle position, able to love what is below and be loved by those above. He takes care of the earth. His swift thought mingles with the elements. . . . His shrewd thought measures the empyrean, as if near at hand. No foggy dew impedes the flight of his intelligence; the compactness of the earth does not impede his digging; nor does the flowing darkness of the deep subaqueous realm frustrate his sight. For he himself is everything at once, and everywhere.

Doesn't this bring Perseus once again to mind? Michelangelo, too, atop his scaffold in the Sistine Chapel, hard at play. The *Corpus Hermeticum* was republished seventeen times during the fifteenth and sixteenth centuries. This, together with the reemergence of pagan myth in general, fostered the full sunshine of the High Renaissance.

Classical philosophic values are not what sparked the Renaissance. The resurgence of deathless poetic instinct did that. I'm talking about the instinct that sets humankind—halfway between animals and gods—at the center of all.

Three Classic Poets

Publius Ovidius Naso, better known as Ovid, was the first pagan poet to come back strong during the Renaissance. His language, Latin, was the same as that of the Catholic Church, so clerically educated Europeans could read him. The poet was something of a rake. He shocked Rome's imperial court, and suffered permanent banishment to far-distant Trebizond on the Black Sea (where he died in 17 A.D.).

From provincial Trebizond, Ovid looked back across his enforced loneliness to the great poets of ancient Greece. He saw that they celebrated nature as a living, breathing trinity. In their legends, he understood, the human, divine, and animal factors merged and separated out again, spinning, scattering clouds of stars, arrows, kisses, feathers, torments, and cornucopiae. Fascinated, Ovid held his breath and leapt boldly out across the abyss, back into the classical sunset. He began his immortal *Metamorphoses* with these lines:

> I mean to tell of bodies changed
> to different forms. I hope the gods,
> who altered them in the first place,
> will see me through.

Ovid took the ancient dragonwheel of animal, human, and divine for his main theme. His verses, winged with a powerful beat, achieved Parnassian sparkle and exuberance. Ovid the Augustan outcast opened up a silvery perspective of pagan myth for succeeding generations to enjoy.

* * *

The Greek farmer-poet Hesiod comes second as a source of pagan lore. Hesiod was roughly contemporaneous with Homer, living no later than the eighth century B.C. Hesiod's view of life was undeniably dark and chill. He lacked Homer's light-footed humanity, but Hesiod had the solemn, unshuttered eyes of a child. A snake was "old Hairless" in his book. A cuttlefish was "the Boneless one, who gnaws his foot in a fireless house."

Hesiod's *Theogony*, a pagan equivalent of the biblical Genesis, argues in effect that immortal lust created our world and still keeps it on course. This poet regarded the joys of gods with bemused, unshockable, and endlessly credulous respect.

Strong were the loins, strong the digestion, of Zeus in particular. Hesiod tells us that after impregnating Metis, the wisest titaness, Zeus slyly ingested her in the form of a fly. Forever imprisoned in Zeus' belly, the titaness gave birth to Athena. She even managed to array the girl in shining armor. Full-grown, the goddess of wisdom then stepped forth from her father's aching head!

By far the greatest poet of the epic lot, Homer ranks third as a wellhead of myth (with Virgil bringing up the rear in his dignified way). Homer portrayed Zeus as having the powers of Superman and the morals of a Borgia. The Zeus whom we meet in *The Iliad* is horny, unbeatable, unbright. Most of *The Iliad*'s human heroes fit the same pattern, it's true, but they possess the added dimension of vulnerability—"tender flesh." They fight, and fall, in strophes appropriate for recital in a warriors' banquet hall.

Contrastingly, *The Odyssey* seems designed for telling beside the kitchen fire. Filled with fairy tale, it's sympathetic to females such as Circe, Calypso, Nausicaa, and, of course, faithful Penelope. It even devotes some lines to Ulysses' verminy old hound, who dies content to see his master one last time. All this suggests that there was not one "Homer," but two. Could one have been a woman?

The Horns of the Prophet

Once in a letter home from Rome, the poet Goethe remarked that until one has planted one's feet on the floor of the Sistine Chapel and gazed up into Michelangelo's vault, one cannot begin to comprehend the full capabilities of the human spirit. I myself was privileged to spend well over a hundred hours contemplating the chapel's barrel-vault from within touching distance (atop a wheeled tower) for film purposes. That was before its ruinous so-called restoration. The experience certainly changed my comprehension of the human spirit. With Michelangelo insistently, tempestuously tugging at my soul day after day, I finally came to realize that the human spirit is neither male nor female. Also, that it does partake of the divine.

During his long life (1475–1564), Michelangelo Buonarroti both suffered and helped to shape the crux and countercrunch of the Italian Renaissance. Educated in Lorenzo de' Medici's household (and tutored, along with Lorenzo's own children, by Poliziano), he was personally acquainted with Marsilio Ficino, Cristoforo Landino, and the great heretical humanist Pico della Mirandola. Their teachings were what inspired his masterpiece at the Vatican.

"Write but don't publish; show but don't tell!" That was a general rule of safety for the humanist circle to which young Michelangelo belonged. The apex of the Sistine ceiling vault stands sixty-eight feet above the floor. The artist adorned the vault's vast surface with an incredibly elaborate, interlocking network of profound and often painful images, poetically veiled. To the casual eye, peering up from below, the whole effect seems orthodox enough, but the barrel-vault of the Sistine seethes with esoteric and even heretical concepts. Indeed, it's a wonder that Church authorities didn't destroy this fresco long ago.

God doesn't sit for portraits, as Michelangelo knew. His "God the Father" at the ceiling's apex (from the "Creation of Adam" forward to the altar wall) is a daimonic emanation of the ineffable. The paternal aspect of this figure is characterized by his venerable beard, plus the erection which juts out his glowing, flowing garment. However, the supreme deity has feminine hips and breasts as well. He, or She, is also the all-nurturing Mother!

Michelangelo's so-called "decorative nudes" (at the corners of each biblical panel) come next in the ceiling's hierarchy of creative forces. Modern critics have sought to explain the "effeminacy" of those half-spiraling etheric figures in terms of the artist's own sexual preference, but that's barbarous. They are pre-sexual beings, active aids to the Creator and, in a word, angels.

The Serpent who tempts Eve in Michelangelo's "Garden of Eden" panel possesses not one but two snake-bodies, closely twined about the Tree of Knowledge. The double serpent's human foreparts reach in opposite directions. One plays the tempter Satan, while his or her twin operates in semi-detached fashion as the avenging angel Gabriel! Here begin the nakedly dichotomous (male/female, temptation/retribution, birth/death) dynamics that drive our lives.

At the next level in the ceiling's hierarchy, prophets and sibyls sit enthroned. These are men and women on a titanic scale, each one imbued with angelic fire, each one destined to help create and recreate the spiritual history of the human race. Homer had done the same, in his or her own style. Michelangelo would do so, too.

When I'm in Rome I always revisit the Greco-Roman marble called "The Dying Gaul" at Rome's Capitoline Museum. It's a tragic piece that paradoxically celebrates undyingness. In this case, the soul-refreshing power of pagan (specifically stoic) idealism. Having paid my respects there, I walk down the hill towards the Foro and turn in at the church of San Pietro in Vincoli, which contains a Michelangelo sculpture of the utmost significance. His marble "Moses" is a legend in itself, fearfully fossilized.

This carving gives fresh force to the Hebrew Prophet's own words (in Deuteronomy):

> When I was gone up into the mount to receive the tables of stone, even the tables of the covenant which the Lord made with you, then I abode in the mount forty days and forty nights, I neither did eat bread nor drink water. . . . And it came to pass at the end of forty days and forty nights that the Lord gave me the two tables of stone, even the tables of the covenant. And the Lord said to me: Arise, get thee down quickly from hence, for thy people, which thou hast brought forth out of Egypt, have corrupted themselves; they are quickly turned aside out of the way which I commanded them: they have made a molten image. Furthermore the Lord spake to me, saying, I have seen this people, and, behold, it is a stiffnecked people: Let me alone that I may destroy them, and blot out their name from under heaven: and I will make of thee a nation mightier and greater than they.

That's the moment Michelangelo chose to portray. He shows us a Moses whose features reflect Jehovah's own volcanic countenance in some degree. This marble figure seems to flame and spiral up, surging, groaning like an earthquake, subsiding even as he rises. For forty days and nights has he conversed with his fiery Lord, and now the volcano tells him that in his absence the Israelites are already whoring after false gods. So Moses turns from Jehovah's light, half rising in his rage to glare down the mountainside, and then checking himself as God threatens to blot out Israel.

Moses is caught between two fires as it were: a faithless people and a vengeful Lord. His left hand clutches his belly, for really bad news does feel just like a kick in the belly at first. Moses' right hand meanwhile strays to his beard and strokes it as he tries, pathethically, to reassure himself. The beard disturbs some critics because it fails to "convince" in the ordinary sense. But Michelangelo meant to pass beyond nature and give a visual hint of the "supernal beard" which figures so large in Pico della Mirandola's translation of *The Cabala*:

> Curls upon curls and all are strong and close and they extend and flow down singly each in its own directions. . . . Curls

heaped upon curls and all are strong and close for breaking, hard as rock and as hardest stone. Until they can make openings in this skull and fountains can flow down beneath the locks, those strong fountains flow forth in separate directions and in separate ways. And because these locks are black and obscure it is written: 'He discovereth deep things out of darkness, and bringeth out to light the shadow of death'. . . . And therefore wisdom floweth forth and procedeth; but it is not the Wisdom of Wisdom for that is quiet and tranquil.

The mixture of stone and water in this precipitously baffling passage recalls Moses' own miraculous striking of water from dry rock. His beard, as carved by Michelangelo, also resembles "hardest stone" at one moment and "fountains" the next. Obviously, cabalistic writings were not expected to make consistent sense, but they were reverently perused in Lorenzo de' Medici's circle, and they doubtless appealed to Michelangelo's searching, unsystematic, half-heretical spirit.

His own beard was very black and wiry, by the way. It became streaked with white only in his extreme old age. And the artist's own wisdom, although apparently great, was clearly not "the Wisdom of Wisdom." Seldom tranquil, that is. Men such as Moses and Michelangelo seem created to lead us to the borders of the Promised Land. They themselves rarely enter in. Peace is not for them.

> When Moses came down from Mount Sinai he held two tablets of the testimony, and he knew not that his face was horned from conversation with the Lord.

That's a passage from Saint Jerome's Vulgate Bible: the one which Michelangelo knew. Confronted with such a clue, the artist may well have remembered Moses' Egyptian heritage, plus the fact that the chief god of the Egyptians was Ammon: a solar deity, horned like a ram. It was said that heroes who conversed with Ammon, and came to be accepted as his sons, also developed horns. Thus, Egyptian sculptors represented Alexander the Great, for example, with horns curving down behind his ears. Thereafter, certain late-classical marble-carvers and coin-designers transposed such horns to the god Zeus himself—as well as to his son Dionysus.

Since Michelangelo was an ardent antiquarian, all this will have been familiar territory. However, the horns which he carved for his "Moses" are not wide-curving evidence of solar might. Instead, they seem to spring newborn from the prophet's brow. Caused by "conversation with the Lord," they've had just forty days and nights in which to grow. The springtime delicacy of their budding stands in terrific contrast to the autumnal head beneath. Moses has seen visions that no human skull could hold; hence, his budding, fragile horns. His head has become a horned altar as it were, a place of sanctuary.

Never in the whole vast panorama of world art, so far as I'm aware, has spiritual illumination been given more telling form. Here, pity and terror stand justified. Here, Michelangelo "discovereth deep things out of darkness, and bringeth out to light the shadow of death."

The shadow that dogs our lives is death, of course. But what is the shadow of death, if not life?

Aeschylus:
Mystery and History

Like the outstretched wings of some enormous, crucified bird, Gela's wheat fields bent glistening to the sun and wind. Old Aeschylus, alone and far from home, tottered along a dirt pathway which meandered down between the yellow Sicilian fields. The playwright's knobby knees lifted and fell. His cane stuttered upon the pebbly ground. His bald pate gleamed. Meanwhile, high overhead, an eagle soared, clutching a tortoise in its talons.

Aeschylus' eyes were no longer much good at seeing things nearby. For that very reason, perhaps, distant things often struck his vision with intensity. Noticing the eagle and the tortoise now, he stopped dead. Never, from that moment, would he advance a single step. Invisible presences—doubt on his right and wonder on his left—seemed to pinion the playwright's skinny wrists. What could be the meaning of the omen which had caught his eye? During the long course of his life he'd seen perhaps a thousand eagles. Not one had carried a tortoise.

In his heart he addressed the victim:

"You!" he thought. "You, with your midair dread, blindly bunched into that swinging house you call a home. It's rather like a shallow skull, your tortoiseshell. Are you aware of how we kill and hollow out your relatives? Yes, we use tortoiseshells to make soundboxes for our lyres. So, as a poet, I'm indebted to your family. And there you go, cowering up inside your shell—like thought in flight—although you occupy a fierce, unfriendly eagle's grip. How long is it since my own thoughts were carried off in such a way? Often in olden days would I be lifted up, and up, and up, for the sake of my plays. That was heady! Half-mad, I felt, although not quite so crazy as I'd been in battle."

Raising his gnarled right fist, Aeschylus knocked at his own ribs. "Heart, open up! Rejoice, can't you?

"When the Persian ambassadors arrived at Athens, demanding tribute in their barbarous tongue, my heart filled with fury. They explained that they'd be satisfied with a small silver casket of Athenian earth plus a bronze jug of water from our river, signifying submission to their Emperor Cyrus. Might as well demand a pound of flesh from our goddess Athena! Well, I could hardly wait for the fight ahead. When it came, on the beach at Marathon, I joined in joyfully. Yet I was awed, and even humbled in a way, to confront such an enemy. Those Persian 'Immortals' would grab for our long spears and break the points across their knees! We kept on coming, though, as Athenians will, gleefully stabbing our splintered shafts into their bowels until the sand and the quietly lapping tide turned crimson. It makes me ill to recall the smell, and yet I enjoyed that fight as much as anything in life!"

In the family vineyard at Salamis, just a few weeks after the victory at Salamis, Aeschylus discovered his own destiny. Remembering, he spoke in his mind again:

"I saw you, Dionysus, that day. In a green robe, sunshine-splashed and spattered with the songs of thieving birds, you came sauntering between the vines. Remember how you passed me by? Then, at the final moment you turned, gazing back in my direction. That's when I nodded my head, to show I understood."

Lifting his left hand, Aeschylus gently slapped his brow.

"I've been your obedient servant all my adult life. Or have I so? From your perspective, Dionysus, things may well have seemed the reverse. Whichever way it happened, anyhow, we did produce some worthwhile plays. You and I created certain scenes—touching Prometheus, for one—to rattle the Athenian brain. We gave our city plenty that was sweet, and still more that was sour, to suck upon!"

The eagle overhead was hungrily seeking a rock on which to drop its prey. Only by smashing the tortoise, could the bird get at its succulent flesh. But the harvest covered and concealed every rock below. Aeschylus meanwhile rambled on:

"Neither war nor poetry, but metaphysics is the proper passion for old men. So tell me then, what lies beyond the physical? If I could ask that eagle in the sky, would he reply?

"If I were an old eagle, instead of an old man, what would I do?

"I'd fly as high as possible, spiraling up towards the noonday sun, to burn away the mist that now obscures my eyes. That done, I'd spiral down again, down the fiery gyre of aether and soft air. Alighting on some remote and wintry mountaintop, I'd rest awhile, chest-deep in snow. Gradually, with my beak, I'd stroke away the weariness afflicting my wings."

Directly overhead the eagle hovered, aimed, and let its burden drop like a downcrashing lyre, to score a perfect hit on the playwright's bald pate. The bird's piercing yellow eyes blinked at the impact. The tortoise broke open as the poet collapsed. The mellow brains of Aeschylus spilled out like honey on the path below.

The wrinkled child of a warrior culture, Aeschylus may have sincerely believed that Marathon represented his finest hour. Already old at the time of his fatal accident (426 B.C.), he had composed his own epitaph in advance. T. G. Higham neatly translated this as follows:

> One Aeschylus, Athenian born,
> Son of Euphorion,
> Lies under this memorial stone
> In Gela's fields of corn.
>
> At Marathon a sacred wood
> His courage will declare,
> Or ask the Medes with braided hair,
> Who tried and found it good.

Patriot though he was, Aeschylus made no bones about the evil price of war. As for the terrible entanglements derived from family love, hatred, and revenge, he wrote of them with sharp psychological realism and extreme bitterness, yet in the noblest possible manner. But according to contemporary accounts, he was also supreme at penning brief, bawdy "satyr-plays"! In short, Aesychylus set Greek drama on its feet, as Shakespeare was to do for English drama in the very distant future. Algernon Charles Swinburne called Aeschylus' "Oresteia" trilogy "the greatest achievement of the human mind." Aeschylus certainly possessed a painfully self-probing intelligence. Witness this fragment:

> They tell it down in Libya—
>
> An eagle, pierced by an arrow,
> regarded the sly, winged object
> protruding from its breast, and said:
>
> "So, not by others
> but by our own plumes,
> are we destroyed."

What intrigues me most about Aeschylus is his ability to seize history in his right hand, legend in his left, and bring the two into concert. No poet, not even Shakespeare, has done that better.

"Manifold and laughable are the sayings of the Hellenes," So Hecataeus of Miletus observed in the sixth Century B.C. His lost book, *Genealogies,* undertook to correct the going folk-wisdom. Was he himself descended from a god, precisely fifteen generations back, as he had been taught? No, Hecataeus, reasoned, the divine seed must have been implanted long before that! And did Herakles really drive the Cattle of the Sun all the way from Spain to the Peloponnese? More likely, Hecataeus opined, he drove them from Epirus, a few hundred miles north.

Herodotus of Halicarnassus, the immortal author of *The Persian Wars,* discreetly expanded this new approach to myth. Did Zeus abduct Princess Europa in the form of a bull? That sounded like bull to Herodotus. Instead, a Cretan pirate must have spirited her away. And did the god Poseidon carve the gorge through which the river Peneius flows? Yes, Herodotus guessed. Poseidon was known as "the Earth-shaker," and nothing short of an earthquake could have done the job.

Aristotle scorned history as being unselective, whereas poetry and myth were not. He thought every gentleman should know what Homer's heroes had accomplished. On the other hand, Aristotle opined, we might as well forget the traitorous activities of an historic figure such as Alcibiades. So much for Thucydides' *History of the Peloponnesan War*. Aristotle had a point, but history would win the day.

About the year 300 B.C., a Sicilian Greek named Euhemerus published a *Sacred History,* which he claimed to have deciphered from inscriptions on a golden pillar far across the Arabian sea. His book, since lost, boldly asserted what Hecataeus, Herodotus, and their successors had often hinted. Myth is nothing but natural history, plus human history, in time-disguised and faith-distorted form. This view has come to be called by the author's name: euhemerism.

Some comic examples spring to mind. Consider Acteon, the peeping-tom whom Artemis transformed into a stag, and who thereupon found himself hunted down by his own pack of hounds. According to Euhemerus, Acteon was a fanatic sportsman, the expense of whose prizewinning hounds "ate him up"! As for Aphrodite, she was a scintillating lady, the all-too-human madame of the world's first prostitution ring! And so on.

Granted that euhemerism encouraged a lot of smudging and fudging down the centuries, it's also provided us with bifocals: glasses through which we may study history plus myth, together and in depth. For instance, it was by trusting the bifocals of Euhemerus that Heinrich Schliemann rediscovered Troy.

Like modern archeology, anthropology also depends upon the historical perspective which Hecataeus and his successors first opened. By applying this perspective to Native American myth, anthropologists have been able to map some Stone Age migrations of tribes.

The poet Robert Graves, for one, was a shameless euhemerist. His admittedly quirky paperback compendium, *The Greek Myths,* remains among the most useful things of its kind. Graves stated his case emphatically in its Introduction:

> The historical and anthropological approach is the only reasonable one: the theory that Chimaera, Sphinx, Gorgon,

> Centaurs, Satyrs and the like are blind uprushes of the
> Jungian collective unconscious, to which no precise meaning
> had ever, or could ever have been, attached, is demonstrably
> unsound. The Bronze and early Iron Ages in Greece were
> not the childhood of mankind, as Dr. Jung suggests. . . .
> Greek mythology was no more mysterious in content than
> modern election cartoons.

In Graves' surprisingly chill eye, the dread Chimaera (which
Bellerophon slew) shrinks to a mere calendar symbol. Her lion
head, goat body, and serpentine tail each "represented a season of
the Queen of Heaven's Sacred year." As for Cheiron and his fel-
low-centaurs, they "were perhaps cognate with the Latin 'cent-
uria,' a war-band of one hundred."

But Graves was a poet, after all, unable to sustain his own
scepticism for long. His deservedly famous work called *The White
Goddess* concerns a pre-Olympian, female deity, the doyen of the
Minoan world, who appears as a mother to the young, a lovely
maiden to men in their prime, and a hag to the dying. Human
sacrifice and the unmanning of men delighted this goddess, and
yet Graves did his antiquarian best to worship at her feet. Invading
Zeus-worshippers, he complained, had overturned her altars one
by one. The Homeric heroes were pigs in his opinion; they didn't
understand women.

The White Goddess never dies. She still puts in occasional ap-
pearances, Graves concluded in all sincerity, as a muse to poets
like himself!

The eternal, overarching divinity whom Graves' favorite goddess personified has gone by many names. Representing "Mother
Nature" in effect, she's still celebrated around the globe. Rival,
patriarchal faiths never entirely overcame the worship of this deity, nor will they ever do so. Witness the special reverence ac-
corded to the Virgin Mary in Roman Catholic and especially in
Eastern Orthodox religious practice. Witness too, the solemn
witch-rites of "white magic" that are still performed here and
there by esoterically inclined devotees.

Here is the prayer by which the hero of Lucius Apuleius' story,
The Golden Ass, achieved his heart's desire and regained human
form:

Blessed Queen of Heaven, whether you are pleased to be known as Ceres, the original harvest mother who—in joy at the finding of your lost daughter Persephone—abolished the rude acorn diet of our forefathers, and gave them bread instead, the fruit of the soil of Eleusis; or whether you accept our veneration as celestial Aphrodite, now adored at sea-girt Paphos in particular, who, at the dawn of creation, coupled the sexes in mutual love and so contrived that each creature continues to propagate its kind forever; or whether you appear as Artemis, the physician sister of Phoebus Apollo, reliever of the birth pangs of women, who is especially worshipped in the ancient shrine at Ephesus; or whether you may prefer the dread role of the Persephone to whom the owl cries at night, and whose triple-visage stares down malicious ghosts, keeping them imprisoned underground; you, who wander through a multitude of sacred groves and find yourself propitiated by so many differing rites; you, whose womanly light gently bathes the battlements of every city, and whose misty radiance nurses the happy seeds under the soil; you, who control the wandering course of the sun together with the very power of his rays: I beseech you—by whatever name, in whatever aspect, and through whatever ceremonies you may deign to have me perform—come to me now in my extreme distress, restore my shattered fortune . . . rid me of this hateful four-footed disguise, return me to my family, make me Lucius once more!

What a lot of history, both natural and religious, the long-eared animal packed into that!

· PART FOUR ·

From Eternity to Here

Beside the path that leads beyond death, wild strawberries are to be found. There they grow in delicious abundance, according to Seneca Indian belief.

When Sky Woman fell down to us through a rift in heaven, the Seneca explain, she'd been picking and eating strawberries. Feeling the ground give way, she naturally clutched at the strawberry plants for support. So it was that she came trailing clouds of strawberries, in glory, to our ever-hungry realm.

Does that legend represent no more than a wishful conceit on some Native American shaman's part? Or, does it encapsulate a mystery of crucial importance for the dying to contemplate? In seed-form, perhaps—a seed too small for reason to handle?

In Part One, I suggested that myth/truth and the mythosphere are actual. In Part Two, I offered a sampling of mythological knowledge-circuits, and in Part Three, I touched upon the mysteries of mythshaping itself. Now in Part Four, I'll try to illustrate my own conclusions, especially as regards myth and the moral realm. Whether Hindu, Judaic, Buddhist, Islamic, or Christian, sacred myth instils compassion of course. But I maintain that compassion is the beginning of the Way for everyone, including scientists. I'm not saying that it's easy. Just a few individuals, here and there, so much as set foot upon the Way. But without compassion there can be no real understanding, no peace, and no wild strawberries at last.

Plato: The Disappearing Handkerchief

S ocrates remarked that "the unexamined life is not worth living." The reverse is also true: the unlived life is not worth examining. That's why my partner and I long ago abandoned our Manhattan careers in order to raise our small children in Greece. The adventure which we set ourselves was this: to try and experience myth and actuality in the same breath.

I recall an afternoon at Hissarlik in Turkey, the hilltop site of ancient Troy. The hill upon which we perched seemed like a giant, grassy skull. This had been very thoroughly dug out and filled in again, first by Schliemann and later by more methodical archeologists who "discovered" no less than seven Troys, one above the other.

We'd come there with a group of scholars on a "Homeric Cruise" organized by a latter-day Croesus to promote classical studies. Two Oxford dons, good friends, were with us at the time. We four didn't talk much; mainly we just sat. Martin West was known for being silent in seven tongues, anyhow. Afterwards, he told me that he'd occupied himself by plotting to get at a hard-to-see Byzantine text in far-off Thessaloniki. As for fierce-faced Regius Professor Hugh Lloyd-Jones, it turned out that he had been composing commentaries on Aeschylus for a coming American lecture, in his head. In my own case, there was wistful yearning for a cold beer. Only my partner Jane sat wide-eyed, unpreoccupied, fully present, in and of the moment.

At one point, a small spiral of dust arose and danced across our view for a minute or more. It brought to mind Homer's messenger goddess: "Iris of the Whirlwind Feet." Dreamily, we contemplated the sleek horses, whole herds of them, grazing along the coastal plain below. "Rich in horses," that was Homer's favorite epithet for Troy! Across three thousand years and more, the horses were still there. My hat blew off. As I ran to catch it, tripping and falling on the uneven turf, I couldn't help being struck by Homer's second-favorite epithet for this place: "windy Troy."

At sunset, as we left, a leering old Gypsy at the gate drew a polished sliver of olivewood from his sleeve. He seemed intent on selling us the useless little thing. It was, he loudly asserted, a "True Fragment from the Trojan Horse!" Wagging their heads in the negative, our learned companions sauntered straight on past the man. My partner paused, looking eager. I paused also, perforce, being behind her. Thinking to save money, I laid the claim that we already possessed a Trojan Horse fragment of our own. The Gypsy expressed shock that I could tell such a fib, especially in this sacred place. Relenting, happily, I purchased the drop-eyed guardian's mythic fragment, his solid lie. We still have it somewhere, an enigmatic souvenir.

In his monumental *Greek Thinkers* (1896), Theodor Gomperz remarked that "nearly our entire intellectual education originates from the Greeks." Therefore, he went on:

> A thorough knowledge of these origins is the indispensable pre-requisite for freeing ourselves from their overwhelming influence. To ignore the past is here not merely undesirable, but simply impossible. Even if you don't know the doctrines of . . . the great masters of antiquity, and even if you never heard their names, you are nonetheless under the spell of their authority. Not only has their influence been extended by those who followed them in ancient and again in modern times, but our entire way of thinking (the logical categories in which it moves and the linguistic patterns which it employs)—all this is no small degree an artifact; and it is, in the main, the product of the great thinkers of antiquity.

Hark to the thunderclap in Herr Doktor's cigar smoke. Don't stop at the ancient Greeks, that's what Gomperz was telling us.

We need to know what they created, as well as where they disagreed, but not for pious reasons. On the contrary, we should study the ancient Greeks in order to pass beyond classical tradition.

Today we can take that thought a long step further. Today I say: don't stop with European or Western culture as a whole. Like the mythosphere, the earth itself is round. Our cultural heritage also is global—nothing less. The time has come to recognize this.

It's what led Jane and me to voyage with our children by freighter through Suez, around India and Southeast Asia to Japan—stopping over at places imbued with Islamic, Hindu, and Buddhist myth. For the same reason, once the children were in college, my partner and I returned to Kyoto on a Japan Foundation Senior Fellowship. There we studied Zen-Buddhism while practicing zazen meditation (under the kindly eye of Masao Abe) for a full year.

It would be untrue to say that these Asian adventures lessened my passion for the classical, but they did cast a new and less favorable light on Plato, who had been my favorite philosopher.

The forms that we actually see and experience, Plato proclaimed, are simply projections of "true" ideas or archetypes existing in eternity. Plato was positing an ideal body of irrefutable truth which stands eternally existent far beyond our mortal ken. This weird, wonderful concept still dominates Western culture and overshadows world civilization.

It's true that Nietzsche, from the poetic side, and Wittgenstein, the analytical genius, pretty well crushed the dry urn of neo-Platonism. And yet, strangely enough, Plato's primary concept continues to be held sacred—in both scientific and religious circles—to this very day. The scientific quest for "Truth" and the religious quest for "Faith" are equally efforts to seize the disappearing handkerchief that Plato waved.

For nearly two and a half thousand years, educated Westerners have followed Plato's lead. Ever since Plato, we've put "Ideas" first, while striving to view the world "Under the Aspect of Eternity." Should we go on this way?

Aesop: His Fall and Rise

He was a spry, distinguished gentleman. She was a beautiful and sexy teenage girl. One summer afternoon they sat together at the top of the Delphian cliff called Hyampeia, swinging their legs and looking down over the gray-blue gorge below.

"Aesop," she said, "these picnics are all very well, but what are you waiting for? You've been with us more than a week. When are you going to put your question to the Oracle?"

"The fact is, Phemonoe, I've been waiting for you to be the Oracle! I want to see you perched on the tripod in Apollo's underground chamber, chewing the laurel leaves."

"That's silly. It makes no difference which girl is on duty. The god speaks through us in a loud male voice. Apollo couldn't care less which one of us he possesses."

"Ah, but what if my question really concerns you, and not the god?"

"In that case it would be impious to consult the Oracle. You'd better say what's on your mind."

Aesop played with a pebble for a while, then tossed it away on the steep air.

"That's dangerous," Phemonoe remarked. "We're not supposed to throw anything down."

Bending his head, Aesop peered over the side. "I want to get married again. Should I?"

"That depends."

"My first wife was a satyr."

"You don't say! I always think of satyrs as being male."

"I loved that girl. She left me, all the same."

"You must have done something to get her goat. Oops! That's a joke."

"She caught me blowing on my fingers, one cold morning, to get them warm. It unnerved her. As a result, she served my porridge much too hot."

"So then what did you do?"

"I blew on the porridge as well, to cool it down. At that point my wife's tail twitched violently—a sure sign of tension. She'd put two and two together, you see."

"No, I don't see at all."

"She'd made up her mind that I must be a sorcerer. I seemed able to blow hot, or cold, as the occasion demanded."

Phemonoe sighed, perhaps with understanding. Casually, it seemed, she undid the clasp at her shoulder and let the top of her linen tunic settle over her hips. Lifting both hands to her neck, she spread her fingers beneath the honey-colored richness of her hair, letting it air.

As a priestess officially "married to Apollo," Phemonoe was privileged to entertain mortal lovers at will. If she were to get pregnant, that would be all right, too. Most of her sister-Oracles had done so. They made a practice of dedicating each love-child, as soon as it arrived, to lifetime service at the sun-god's shrine. From that point on, the temple organization took care of everything. Surely, Aesop had informed himself concerning her availability. He seemed a clever fellow, smart enough to take advantage. Virile, too, apparently. He must be sixty at least, she told herself; and yet—glancing sideways into his lap—she noticed a distinct bulge beneath his linen robe.

"Married to a satyr!" she said now. "That must have been swell while it lasted. Tell me, why didn't you and your wife simply sit down and talk things over?"

"We should have. All I needed to do was to explain the physical realities involved. My breath-temperature was warmer than my chilled fingers, and cooler than the hot porridge—yet constant in itself."

"That's neat!"

"But what I actually said was 'Please pass the cream.'"

"I love cream."

"The next thing I knew, my satyr-bride had fled! Clean out of the back door and away up the pasture toward home she ran, the lovely little bounder. Home to her mountain mother." While he was speaking, Aesop slyly stretched himself out sideways. He came to rest on his back, with his head pillowed in Phemonoe's lap. Indulgently, she smiled down between her breasts at him."

"What do you think you're doing?"

"Getting ready to bell you, my dear."

Far below Phemonoe, a pair of eagles wheeled in the updraft. She spread her feet to frame them, watching idly, as one might gaze upon a pair of goldfish in a pool. "Bell me?" She said now. "Is that something I'd enjoy?"

"Could be. Once upon a time, the mice convened a council of war against their common enemy, the cat. Various strategies were proposed, only to be voted down. Finally a philosophical old mouse suggested tying a warning-bell around the cat's neck. If she were 'belled' they could always hear her coming, and escape in time."

"That sounds sensible."

"The mice agreed with you. The oldster's motion was applauded, approved, and passed unanimously. Then, in the ensuing silence, someone squeaked: 'Which distinguished member of this august assembly shall we appoint?'"

"Appoint for what, Aesop? I don't get it."

"Appoint to bell the cat, which would be no pushover."

"I should think not! How could a mouse ever bell a great ferocious cat?"

"There you go, Phemonoe!"

Overcome with annoyance, Apollo's priestess scrambled angrily to her feet. In the process, she accidentally pitched her friend over the cliff. Just at first he seemed able to hover on the updraft, like a dry leaf. Curious, the splendid eagles spiraled around the falling man. Aesop kept craning his neck about like a sightseer all the way down, until it broke.

The rest, as they say, is history. Aesop turned out to be far more important than Phemonoe had guessed. His death caused a scandal. When the priests of Delphi asked their own Oracle what to do, Apollo suggested offering a huge recompense in silver to Aesop's heirs. But it seems he had no descendants; and for a time no one stepped forward. Eventually, however—as Herodotus tells us—a man named Iadmon successfully pressed his claim to the blood-money. Iadmon was able to prove that his deceased grandfather, on the island of Samos, had once owned Aesop and had freed the fabulist from slavery.

In the meantime, Delphi passed a new house rule which was destined to stand for centuries. In future, the authorities decreed, all priestesses of the Oracle must lead chaste lives. Furthermore, no lady under fifty need apply for the job.

These events occurred during the mid-sixth century B.C., so Aesop must have been aware of Pythagoras the mathematician and Salmoxis the Thracian magus, who were also connected with Samos. Among Aesop's other contemporaries were the free-booting bard Alcaeus, the lesbian lyricist Sappho, and most of the pre-Socratic philosophers. Contrasted with those great bears of culture, however, Aesop seems a drily cackling, far-flying, grayly elusive goose.

Although we don't possess a single tale that we can swear is of Aesop's own invention, no one doubts that he invented the fable form—or that he gave it a tremendous push from his clifftop perch of long, long ago. Among his many classic debtors was the Roman poet Phaedrus, a contemporary of Jesus, who committed 150 fables to verse. Another was Valerius Babrius, who flourished in Syria during the second century of the present era.

William Caxton, the great fifteenth-century British printer and translator, was first to render Aesop in our language. Jean de la Fontaine (1621–1693) carried the Aesopian tradition to its French apogee. Gotthold Ephraim Lessing published his collection in 1759, with a preface which helped spark the German Enlightenment. Today, new editions of Aesop's fables are being read in every language and in every land. They're regarded as "children's literature," however—too simple-minded for us oh-so-clever adults.

Like the "Jataka Tales" of Buddhist India, and the Islamic Turkish "Tales of the Hodja," Aesop's fables may appear trivial at first glance. Are they so? Having read Aesop along with the Jataka and

Hodja stories to my small children, many times over, I must say that the whole lot wear very well.

Aesop took the basic geometries of social existence for his subject. By making animals act out these comic and/or cruel patterns, he set social behavior at one remove, while simultaneously bringing the animals closer to our consciousness. Observing our own pointy snouts or vain feathers or mean and foolish ways in Aesop's brilliant little mirrors, we smile—ruefully, it's true. That's better than to live in frozen horror of our condition, as many do.

I picture the evolution of human consciousness in the shape of an hourglass. In the prehistoric top half, humanity regarded itself as one among many animal tribes, and as being imbued with many different forms of animal intuition. But now, in the bottom half, our animal brotherhood is forgotten. We consider ourselves heirs to a large variety of historic civilizations. We've been branded, bonded, and redivided by thousands of debatable ideas. Aesop pulls us back up through the hourglass of evolution, helping us to sense the fact that we're still cousins to the animals—alike in that respect.

"Each academic species has evolved its own language, so interdisciplinary communication is rare and fitful. By exploring such distinct cultures, however, we learn to challenge evidence and patiently puzzle out our own answers." So said Nobel-prize-winning chemist Dudley Herschbach in his 1992 Harvard-Radcliff Phi Beta Kappa Oration. "Try it out," he challenged. "Think of yourself as a Dolphin oracle and ask about any issue of the day. Try problems involving differences in gender, race, religion, political persuasion, national identity, or the like. . . . It can only do humankind good to become more aware that along with the dolphins and other incredible creatures, we really belong to a much wider universe of the mind, it could be called mindkind."

Aesop assumed as much, but it's good to hear the old idea resurfacing once more.

The Tale of the
Jade Emperor's Mother

C hinese myth, like the Greek, delights in irony. The reason, I think, is that both the ancient Greeks and the ancient Chinese were philosophically inclined. They subjected the gods themselves to pinches, prodding, laughter, and scratching. Witness this Mandarin finger-exercise:

The Jade Emperor of Heaven has always exhibited paternal affection for the inhabitants of lands below his realm. One evening the Emperor dropped in at his old mother's palace with a small request. "Mother," he said, "I've been called away on business for three days. While I'm gone, would you be so kind as to answer the people's prayers that drift up from below?"

"Certainly, my son. It will give me something to do."

The next morning, the Jade Emperor's mother stepped down from her rainbow palace and mounted a soft cloud. Swiftly she sailed away across the land to see what needed doing. As she was passing over the Yangtse, she heard a ship's captain pray: "Heavenly Father, I've got a cargo of bananas here. Please send a wind to boost this ship to port before they all turn black!" So she made the wind blow briskly for him. Soon afterwards, however, she heard another man pray: "Heavenly Father, save my orchard. Stop the wind! It's breaking branches and blowing all my peaches to the ground."

The Jade Emperor's mother returned in some confusion to her palace. The following morning she set off again, however, with her customary good will. It wasn't long before she heard someone pray: "Heavenly Father, send rain so I can sow my beans today!" She ordered down a nice, heavy rain, but then on her way home she heard someone else pray: "Heavenly Father, save my ginger crop! In this rain, the whole lot will rot."

The Jade Emperor's mother could bear it no longer. Developing a sick headache, she spent the third day at home in her palace. That evening her son returned and came to see how she was getting on. With many sighs, his mother recounted her prayer-answering efforts, such as they were. She was so sorry, she said, but the job had been too much for her.

"It's not all that difficult, really," the Jade Emperor responded in a kindly tone. "You should send a strong wind over the rivers, and a gentle breeze upon the orchards. Have rain fall in the night-time to nurture bean seeds, and let the sun shine during the day for ginger-drying."

The Jade Emperor's mother understood at once. "But," she inquired with a smile, "why didn't you tell me before?"

The Ocean-Warming Piglet

L ong ago, on the far side of our planet, there lived a farmer named Li-pin. His home was a straw hut close by the glittering South China Sea. Li-pin's only companion was a wrinkled piglet, as scrawny as himself. He treated the piglet tenderly, played games with it, and spoke to it as if to a child. One day he said:

"Dear beast of mine, I'm glad you're not growing any bigger, for I love you as you are. But on the other hand, I feel guilty that I can't feed you properly. There's seldom any food on my table; hence, no scraps for you. So there's only one thing to do. For your own welfare, I must try to sell you! Failing that, I'll simply give you away to the next rich person who comes along."

"Don't do it!" the piglet squealed.

"What? You speak Chinese? This is wonderful! But why haven't you ever before replied to my idle chatter?"

"That's the reason," said the piglet. "Idle chatter requires no response. Just now, however, you threatened to dispose of me. As I said, you mustn't."

"Have no fear. I wouldn't dream of it now. You're my only friend, and you can talk! So we'll starve together."

"That won't be necessary. I want you to take me down to the shore, put me in a pot, and boil me there."

"What a dreadful idea! Out of the question."

"Listen. I'm what they call an 'ocean-warming pig.' My kind never grows fat, or tough; never reaches maturity. But when we're boiled in a pot, the ocean boils up as well; it turns to steam, whereupon the riches of the sea-bottom stand revealed."

"Then, if I boil you we'll be rich! Or I will, anyhow. You'll just be dinner, right? I won't even consider it."

"Believe me," snorted the piglet, "I can take the heat."

After some further discussion and considerable soul-searching on Li-pin's part, he allowed himself to be persuaded. Carrying the piglet under one arm and a cauldron under the other, he thoughtfully descended to the shore. It wasn't long before Li-pin had gathered some driftwood, made a fire, set the pot over it, and then—with many tearful apologies—stuffed his perfectly willing companion down into the pot.

Instantly, the sea boiled up. Swirling steam obscured the retreating waves. Hot bursting bubbles spattered the rapidly widening beach. Then came a vision lovelier than anything Li-pin had imagined in his whole life. A green-clad, teenage girl, with goldfish earrings and flowing purple hair, came running up to him over the sand. "Stop boiling!" she cried. "My father's palace will collapse!"

Li-pin guessed right away that the girl must be a daughter of the Dragon King who inhabits the depths of the southern ocean, but he pretended otherwise. "I'm just sitting here minding my own business and cooking my pig," he mumbled. "What do I know about palaces?"

"Please!" the girl implored.

"Please what?"

"You know very well." She paused. "Am I attractive?"

"More than heaven itself."

"Then get that cursed pig out of the pot!"

"What for?"

"Do as I say, quickly. If you do, then I will marry you for a year and a day!"

No sooner had Li-pin's companion heard those words than it scrambled happily up out of the cauldron. With infinite self-sacrificing courage, the ocean-warming piglet had done its work. Although the animal glowed rosy-pink, it appeared none the worse for its ordeal. Yet at this point—while the southern sea returns to normalcy—the creature vanishes from our story.

That's by no means the end, however. The Dragon King's daughter had come through beautifully, dashing up the hot beach to remonstrate with Li-pin in her father's time of need. Now she proved to be as good as, or even better than, her word! The poor farmer spent a joyful year in her company, during which he learned many wonderful secrets.

Neither Li-pin himself nor his ocean-warming heart of hearts could possibly have guessed what those secrets would be. Did they have preexistence (not to mention post-existence) in eternity? Or did they spontaneously manifest themselves, like the foam of a wave or the bloom on a country hedge in spring? Or were the wonderful secrets generated—as I myself prefer to imagine—by surprising love between the Dragon King's daughter and Li-pin?

Po Chu-i's Mirror Poem

Like the legendary Li Pin, the poet Po Chu-i was also reputed to have lived for a year and a day with the Dragon King's daughter. That reputation may have been based on a noted poem from his ink-brush. Here it is, in my rendering:

When my Princess parted from me
she left her bronze mirror,
like a pond with no lotus,
no reflection of her.

She's been gone so long.
I open her mirror-box.
Dust obscures the bronze.
I brush it off—

What's this?
My withered face.

Turning the mirror over,
I feel worse than before.
On the back: a dragon pair
coupling cloudlike in midair.

Isn't it strange how much romantic literature—whether Oriental or Occidental—concerns the aftermath of love and the wistful dynamics of loss? Inspiration's glorious and stormy onset appears far more difficult to celebrate.

When one has been unhorsed from Pegasus, or the Dragon King's daughter slips away beneath the waves once more, what

171

should one do then? The romantic option is to mourn in a personal way. The classical option is different. Namely, to mold from the amorphous churn of bereavement a fresh being, a self-born figure, eloquent and gleaming with compassion. In other words a "Muse," such as the ancient poets invoked.

Socrates' Secret Dream

"**I**s any man wiser than Socrates?" An Athenian pilgrim once put that question to the Delphic Oracle. "No man!" came the instant response.

Returning joyfully to Athens, the pilgrim told his friend Socrates the news.

The philosopher was appalled. "I said to myself, what can the god mean?" he later explained. "What is the interpretation of his riddle? For I know that I have no wisdom, small or great." Socrates proceeded to scour Athens, questioning high and low, in hopes of finding someone wiser than himself—to no avail. Had she been a man, his dear friend Aspasia could have filled the bill. But Aspasia no longer lived. So Socrates concluded that the Oracle was irrefutable.

"The man is wisest who, like Socrates, knows that his wisdom is in truth worth nothing."

I suppose that if Aesop were telling this, Socrates would be cast as a pesky mockingbird who darts about Athens making fools of the lion, the fox, the wolf, and so on. Inevitably, they gang up on him; and that's what happened. Socrates was put on trial for his life. He could have gotten off. However, something which he described as an inner "Voice" commanded him to relate the whole hilarious story of his wisdom-search. Nobody laughed. Fatally offended, the jury condemned him to death.

While awaiting execution, intriguingly enough, Socrates occupied himself with turning some of Aesop's fables into verse. But it's never been suggested that he passed his verses on. "Words, once enscrolled," he observed, "cannot defend themselves." And so, like Aesop before him, Socrates left no written legacy. We know the *Dialogues* that Plato put in his mouth, and we have Xenophon's reminiscences of the man, but what transpired in Socrates' secret heart? There's no way to get near that, except on wings of fantasy.

Our curtain rises to reveal a crypt-like prison interior at night. Socrates lies stretched out beneath a barred alcove window. His coverlet is so short as to expose his feet. Moonlight filters dimly through the window to illuminate an iron ring, bolted to the wall, from which a chain loops down to a shackle on Socrates' ankle. A lovely woman coalesces from the moonlight. She's diaphanously gowned in her own flowing hair, mingled with swirling shadows. Seating herself on the broad stone shelf where Socrates lies asleep, she touches the shackle. At once it dissolves; the chain hangs loose from the wall. Socrates awakens, sits up, swings his feet to the floor and joyfully embraces her.

SOCRATES

Aspasia! You're . . . a dream, aren't you?

ASPASIA

Am I?

SOCRATES

But you've been dead for twenty years! And now you're—

ASPASIA

What, darling?

SOCRATES

(Kisses her eyelids, her nose, her lips, her neck, and runs his hands through her hair.)

You're young and warm again! The same as when we were first together. Oh, how I've missed you, longed for you.

ASPASIA

I know.

SOCRATES

You do? I myself never realized the force of my yearning, until now—like an underground river! What's happened? Did I die in my sleep? Is that why we're together once more?

ASPASIA

No, my dear, you didn't die in your sleep. I've come alive in your sleep.

SOCRATES

Why?

ASPASIA

I'm not sure. Let's find out.

SOCRATES

(Gleefully).

It's like old times! I have a theory. I think you've come to encourage me. Tomorrow, I must die.

ASPASIA

Yes, that's part of it.

SOCRATES

I'm determined to die well. Listen. When you were a child, did you fear the dark?

ASPASIA

Not that I can recall.

SOCRATES

I did. I was terrified. Not of darkness itself, but of some totally unknown, unknowable Something.

ASPASIA

(Musingly.)

I've never before heard you mention your childhood.

SOCRATES

It wasn't all that happy. But the point is this. My childhood fear of the dark enables me to sympathize with adult fears of death.

ASPASIA

(Nodding.)

Almost everyone fears death. They've no idea what lies beyond it. That's why they turn to jelly at the very time when they should be strongest.

SOCRATES

Yes, and that's why it's important, after all, to leave a decent example of dying well.

ASPASIA

(Smiling.)

I agree. Nothing that we can do is better calculated to help our fellow-creatures in time of need.

SOCRATES

(With an adoring look, takes her hand in his.)

Nothing except coming to life again, as you have done.

ASPASIA

(Caressingly.)
Can you tell the reason?

SOCRATES

Love. It plays like beating wings between my heart and yours.

ASPASIA

Our love began in bodily desire. It grew from there.

SOCRATES

Pericles came between us.

ASPASIA

I loved you both. Do you imagine that a woman can love only one man at a time?

SOCRATES

I'm not that naive. What I meant was, he came between us in the practical sense. So we settled for the subtler delights of conversation, including philosophical discourse. While it lasted, talking beat sex.

ASPASIA

And then I died—

SOCRATES

Not really. You've never left me.

ASPASIA

That's true. The voice that spoke in your heart, warning you what not to do—

SOCRATES

Guiding my actions, day by day—

ASPASIA

I was that voice.

SOCRATES

I never guessed!

ASPASIA

At your trial, I kept silent. But only because I agreed with everything you said and did.

SOCRATES

Everything?

ASPASIA

(Laughs.)
Even the silly parts. People should be silly, once in a while. It's natural.

SOCRATES

So is asking questions. But that's what brought me here.

Why, oh why, did Apollo's Oracle proclaim me the wisest of men?

ASPASIA

The god had recognized himself in you.

SOCRATES

How can that be?

ASPASIA

For most of your life, you've done battle in Apollo's service. At all times, you defend the god who cannot lie.

SOCRATES

Yes.

ASPASIA

In the process, you've slowly re-created your own soul!

SOCRATES

(Awed.)

I re-created my own soul?

(Stretching out again, he shuts his eyes.)

ASPASIA

You are godlike now.

(The prisoner sleeps. Bending low, Aspasia touches her lips to his brow.)

Chuang Tzu, Vishnu, and Manu

Do you remember Rodin's famous bronze called "The Thinker"? Resting his chin on his fist, this muscular male nude frowningly contemplates the ground. There's a cast of Rodin's heroic intellectual figure near the entrance to Kyoto's Museum of Modern Art. I went there one day with Masao Abe and asked him what he thought of the statue. "Pursuing illusion!" my teacher exclaimed. He meant to tease, and we both laughed, but my laughter was somewhat pained. "The Thinker" has nothing in common with orthodox Asiatic sculptures of "Buddha," that's true. "Buddha" serenely contemplates his interior world, whereas "The Thinker" intently follows a train of thought. Aren't both things worth doing?

The Oriental pursuit of mindless mind, or "Emptiness," sharply contrasts with our Occidental delight in reason and "Form." Can the two ideals ever be reconciled? No, but nothing prevents us from striving to achieve both.

Once Chuang Tzu and his friend Hui were standing on a bridge across the river Hao, gazing down into the clear water. "Look there," said Chuang. "See those minnows darting about! That's what they like."

"You're not a fish," Hui objected, "so how do you know what they like?"

"Hmm. You're not me," Chuang replied, "so how do you know I don't?"

Hui had a quick answer to that. "What you say is accurate. I certainly don't know what you know, since I'm not you. By the

178

same token, since you're not a fish, you can't possibly tell what fish enjoy."

Chuang sighed briefly. "Let's get back to your original question. You asked me how I knew what fish like. So when you put the question, you assumed I did know the answer, and I do. I know it by standing here on this bridge, gazing down into the clear waters of the Hao."

That anecdote has engendered endless fuss and flurry, not to mention thrust and parry, in East and West alike, for century after century. Why? Chuang Tzu, the inscrutable Chinese sage of the story, flourished more than twenty-four hundred years ago. Thus, his life overlapped with Plato's in the time-dimension. But philosophically, as well as in the space-dimension, they stood worlds apart.

Plato insisted that philosophy and poetry are always at war with one another. The power behind philosophy is reason, whereas the power behind poetry is intuition—Chuang Tzu's forte. He knew what the minnows were feeling, but even so his assertion offended the commonsense of his friend. So Hui responded with "Hooey!", and the debate was on.

Scholars have treated it as an exercise in semantics, replete with fishily darting linguistic twists. Mythologist Wendy Doniger took a professional look at the dispute (in *Other People's Myths*) as follows:

> All animals can be mythical beasts [and] the fish is such an animal. Christianity and Hinduism share the same image of the ever-expanding divine fish; the fish eating the fish ad infinitum, together with its variant, the fish biting its tail . . . a symbol of infinity. The fish that swallows the ring or the cast-off child only to reveal it years later, becomes a symbol of memory, of the persistence of the past, perhaps of the unconscious. . . . When the Chinese sages speak of the fish therefore, they are not only communicating with fish from the bridge (between two different species) but communicating with one another through fish, through the deep level of memory from which we fish things up into our conscious thought.

That's all very interesting, to be sure. Yet I myself prefer to take the sage's story straight. Here's my own theory: I think Chuang Tzu gazed down through his own reflection in the river Hao. I believe he watched the minnows flex and fling their tiny silver selves in nervily harmonious unison, handful by handful, to illuminate the darkly wavering reflection of the sage's own heart-region. He really did understand what they were feeling. Just as he himself enjoyed their many-dimensioned play, so they too must be having a good time! Furthermore, by sympathizing with the minnows, Chuang repeated—at that very moment—the mythic action of Manu, the First Man, who saved Vishnu in minnow form, and whom the god rescued in turn.

The god Vishnu once took the form of a tiny minnow. The minuscule glimmer of the swimming god caught Manu's eye. Instantly, the First Man scooped it up in one hand.

To save the divine fish from predators larger than itself, Manu kept it alone in a water dish. When it outgrew the dish he transferred it to a jar, then to a barrel, then to a pool, then to a pond, then to a lake, and finally to the ocean, since by that time Vishnu had grown sufficiently great in girth to swallow any other fish.

Long afterwards a great flood arose, inundating the shores of the world. As Manu ran away inland, the billowing surge overtook him and swept him far backwards down the watery abyss. He would have drowned, but Vishnu—who was now Leviathan—arrived in time to save him. So Manu rode out the flood in comfort on Vishnu's back, which seemed a sizeable floating island, a Paradise, or a New World rising where the old had disappeared.

Psyche: All for Love

C oncord, Psyche's daughter, came home from school in tears. Taking the child in her arms, Psyche asked what had gone wrong. "They call me a love-child, as if that were something bad," Concord wailed. "Is it, Mother? And here's another thing. They laugh because I don't have any father!"

"Listen, darling, every single child in this world has a father and a mother, too. That's so for all your schoolmates, and for you as well. But some parents have things to do which take them far away."

"Why, Mother? I don't understand."

"Neither do I, not completely. I've baked some cookies for us. Here's your cup of cambric tea. Let's sit down quietly and I'll explain where you came from."

"Oh, Mother! I know perfectly well that I came out of your belly."

"Yes, but that's not even half the story. Now, if you promise not to interrupt, I'll tell what really happened."

"I'll be still as a mouse. I love you, Mother, and besides I'm dying to know."

"All right, then. Here I go—

"I met your father through some enchantment, never seeing him face to face at first. He used to speak to me most lovingly. We slept together. . . .

"Like a fool, being only sixteen at the time, I told my older sisters what was going on. They frightened me half to death by saying that for all I knew I might be married to some horrible serpent! 'Tonight,' they suggested, 'wait until your invisible husband falls asleep. Then light the lamp at your bedside, and take a look! Who knows what nastiness you may find. In fact, you'd better have a sharp knife handy, to slay the monster who's slithered into your bed.'

"Late that night, I lit the lamp and held it up over my sleeping husband's head. No snake was he, but a heavenly-looking youth, the gentlest and sweetest of all the gods, Eros himself! I recognized Aphrodite's son by his loveliness, the smile of mischief on his sleeping face, and, of course, his softly folded wings.

"The knife in my hand also recognized him. In shame, the blade turned from his pulsing throat. Even my oil lamp welcomed the sight of Eros. Joyfully, its flame leapt up, illuminating the whole room.

"Startled awake, Eros sat up in bed. As he did so his shoulder struck the lamp, knocking it from my grasp. The hot oil spilled down upon his chest, sizzling, as my dear god cried out in pain. Then he was gone, vanished. . . .

"I would have died of grief, but for one thing. Our child—you, Concord—began growing inside of me. I knew that it would not be right to do away with both of us. Alone, barefoot, I walked the world in search of my husband. Eventually, my quest led to his mother's palace.

"Aphrodite greeted me roughly. In fact, she slapped me and even kicked me. Then, as I lay weeping on the floor, she stood with her hands on her naked hips, laughing herself sick. The guttural gloom and ceaseless crash of a cascading waterfall was in her laughter, plus the dim bedlam-bleat of malevolent sheep. The goddess is stunning to look at, but horrible in anger. However, she finally cooled down and granted me permission to speak. When I implored her to let me see my husband, the goddess agreed. If I could pass three tests before sunset, she said, I would hold Eros in my arms again!

"But, Aphrodite warned, if I failed to pass the tests, she would set her watchdogs—named Anxiety and Grief—upon me. Those dogs were specially trained, she explained, to tear pregnant, shameless young ladies limb from limb! With that, Aphrodite poured quantities of wheat, barley, millet, lentils, beans, poppy seeds, and vetch out onto the floor. She stirred them all together with her toes into a single heap. Before sauntering from the room, she ordered me sort to the whole business back into separate piles again!

"Squatting down at once I made my fingers fly amongst the mess, but after a minute or two I realized it was no use. Even if I had all day to do it in, I couldn't possibly complete the task alone. Tears came to my eyes. Then, through my tears, thousands of tiny ants appeared! Plainly intent upon rescue, they set to work sorting and carrying as fast as they could go. They scurried furiously about until—after a quarter of an hour—the wheat, barley, millet, lentils, beans, poppy seeds, and vetch stood neatly arranged in seven heaps, like separate planets all around me. I tried to thank the ants. Never pausing, they hurried out of sight again, under the floorboards.

"Minutes later, Aphrodite returned. 'Here's your next little job!' she cried, grabbing my hair and pulling me to the window. 'See the sheep in the shade of those trees? There, on the far side of the garden brook. Pretty, aren't they? Go bring me a hank of their golden wool!'

"Obediently, I hurried out. Crossing the greensward, I stepped down into the shallow, slow-moving stream. As I did so, a frog on a lilypad croaked warningly: 'Those sheep are man-eaters!'

"Astonished, I stood still, staring across at the golden glimmer of the sheep among the trees. Seeming peaceful, they moved like sunbeams in a shuttered room. 'Nonsense,' I told the frog. 'Sheep don't eat us. They themselves resemble humans, after all.'

"'You eat them,' the frog reminded me. Grinning, it snapped a fly out of the breeze. The same breeze brought the baaing of the sheep to my ears. They sounded bloodthirsty, somehow; not like ordinary sheep at all. Stooping down, I gazed into the frog's liquidly bulging, sundial eyes. 'The sheep sound decent,' I lied, uncertain what to do.

"'That's so.' the frog replied. 'Even the cry of the murderous cranes, which happens to freeze my blood, is musical.'

"Glancing up again, I noticed some briars which overhung the far bank. Golden bits of wool hung caught upon the thorns. The sheep had evidently brushed against those briars while drinking from the stream. So, wading across, I hastily plucked the harvest of the briars. Then I splashed back again, thanked my friend the frog for his warning, and ran to the palace with a good armful of golden wool.

"Aphrodite lay on her chaise longue, naked as usual, like a funerary statue of polished marble. The love godess had been ugly to me but now, seeing her this way, my heart swelled and pounded unexpectedly. Kneeling, I laid the wool at her feet on the couch, but she kicked it away. Fearfully, I glanced up. Her expression was distant, cold. 'I'm not myself this afternoon,' she murmured. 'However, you've done well.'

"I nodded, for I couldn't think what to reply.

"Wearily, softly, like discordant music, the goddess rambled on: 'I'm fit as a lyre most of the time. Well-tuned, you understand. Right now my worries have me feeling itchy, hoarse, and faint. My temperature has dropped. Feel my toes, girl.'

"They were frighteningly chill. 'All I need,' Aphrodite said, 'is a cupful of water from the river Styx.'

"'I'll get it for you, goddess,' I promised. 'That is, if I possibly can.'

"She nodded. 'You'll find a small silver cup on the rim of the well in the yard. Follow the left-hand path which leads up through the woods. Soon you'll hear the roar of a cascade. The blessed Styx, the silver river of darkness, will draw you on.'

"Climbing the path I felt almost happy. Divine Aphrodite was counting on me! As I approached through the pine trees, the murmur of the cascading Styx swelled to a low, throaty roar. 'Sought nought, caught nought, wrought nought, thought nought, ought nought, taught nought!' the river repeated in a rushing tone.

"My path ended at the edge of a mossy cliff. The rapids foamed along some ten or fifteen feet below where I stood. There was no way for me to climb down and dip my cup in the stream!

"Then I heard a warm, warbling song, which went something like this: 'Fling ought, cling ought, ring ought, swing ought, wing ought, bring ought, sing ought!'

"The source of the song was a small bird, a water-ouzel which hopped from rock to rock occasionally dipping beneath the surface so that the river bubbled up across his back. As I stood watching—so near my goal and yet so far—the water-ouzel paused and cocked a merry eye in my direction as if to say: 'Come down! Join the fun!' Well, I shrugged and shook my head to let him know it wasn't possible. The water-ouzel seemed to understand. Emerging from the stream, he flew up and around me, then dropped to rest upon my wrist.

"'Silly bird," I said. "Why perch on me? I'm not a tree, just a girl in trouble."

"The water-ouzel shook the transparent drops from his sober, coal-hued plumage. 'What sort of trouble?'

"'Aphrodite sent me. She's feeling ill. A cupful of water from the Styx would set her right again, but there's no earthly way for me to scoop it in.'

"'Just hold out your cup,' the bird advised. 'Let the spray fill it up!'

"When I got back, Eros was there! As Aphrodite drained the silver cup, your dear father embraced me. And then I heard the goddess laugh, happy laughter this time. The scurry of a thousand ants, the croaking of a frog, and the song of a water-ouzel as well, joined in Aphrodite's good laughter. Fit as a lyre once more, she sounded well-tuned for sure. The gift of the spray of the river of darkness, which I—a mere mortal—had brought, made a big difference!

"So you see, Concord, sweet daughter of mine, we can be of some use to the divine."

What is it that nature challenges and tests to the utmost? And who does Eros, the god of love, embrace with his refulgent, healing ambience? The answer is the same in both cases. Namely Psyche, the human soul. Her trials appeared insurmountable at first. She found help, however, and finally the soul's loving courage prevailed. Regarding humankind's immortal soul, I set one finger to my lips in silent awe.

"Strange Minstrelsy"

I have a talkative mindset, but when I do "zazen meditation" my interior dialogue fades out. For a brief while, I hardly think at all in the rational sense: I simply "am." Only afterwards do I become aware of having embraced something beyond my ordinary consciousness. At once, the memory wavers, but the experience itself has been more vivid than ordinary "waking" existence.

People who practice meditation are not the only ones to experience this sort of thing. It may be rare, but it does occur in all our lives. Such private events are neither "objective" nor "subjective": they're beyond the pale of logic and the purview of reason. Hence, like dreams they decline to be plainly grasped and accurately recalled, let alone described or shared.

Every now and then, however, a poet may catch something of their quality—on the wing, as it were. Take for instance the following lines from the siren-spirit chorus to Euripides' *Helen*. J. T. Sheppard's translation may seem old-fashioned, but it best conveys the hypnotic lyricism of the original. If one makes the experiment of putting oneself in a contemplative mood and then reciting the verses aloud, something strange may happen.

> I had washed my robes of red
> And on fresh green rushes spread
> In the meadows by the cool
> Darkly gleaming waterpool
> For the golden sun to dry,
> When I heard a voice, a cry;
> Such a cry as ill would suit

The happy music of my lute;
And I wondered what might be
The cause of that strange minstrelsy,
So sad, and yet so wondrous clear.

It might have been some Naiad flying,
With a cry of sudden fear,
Or in secret cavern lying
Desolate, the ravished bride
of Pan upon the mountain-side.

The washing of the red garments, the setting out to dry, the gleaming sun on the cool of the pool, in fact this whole chorus can work upon and simultaneously still one's consciousness, so that one feels weirdly "inside of" the whole thing. Yet even in Arcadia comes that sudden cry! One wants to find out where it came from and, if possible, to help. So, two thirds of the way through, the delicious wholeness of this poetic experience dissolves into a sort of rainbow shimmer. All is not lost, however, if one fixes full and instantaneous attention upon the cry itself—"so sad and yet so wondrous clear."

If mountains be the bones of this planet, the seas her blood, the forests her hair, and so on, as ancient Chinese and other sages have said, then what are we to her? Can it be that animal and human beings serve Planet Earth in somewhat the same fashion that our own sense-organs and mental-play minister to ourselves? If that is true, then personal death becomes nothing but punctuation in a continuing biography of the earth. Then we are not, after all, destined for heaven or doomed to hell. There's no further need to stand on tiptoe, at the beck and call of some arbitrary "high power" who commands obedience from afar.

This is fanciful, yes, a personal myth which tends to inculcate humility and community, minus the vice of submissiveness. It also banishes nightmares of hellfire or worse, such as nonbeing down endless icy space-time. For we are rooted here, as it were. We serve as nerve-ends and intellectual outriders to the spherical, spinning goddess who dreamed us up in the first place!

The hot blaze of a summer noon, blue skies, balmy breezes,

screeching winds, thunder clouds, torrential rains, immense calm, brightness falling from the air as snow—these plus a thousand more phenomena comprise our planet's natural breath. We're all aware that this surrounds, protects, nourishes, and energizes the world "out there." The mythosphere does all that too, but for the world "in here."

It's a world beginning in dreams and, with them, responsibilities. It's our own world that we keep reporting back, unbenownst even to ourselves, for good or ill.

The legendary beings whom I love best tackled reality straight—not "Under the Aspect of Eternity" but "Under the Aspect of the Instant." They never pursued their own bliss in self-important ways. Rather, they creatively addressed the immediate demands which compassion placed upon them. I'm talking about the deities, the people and the animals who sprang most vividly from the wings of eternity in order to help out here and now. Psyche, for example, and her wild helpers, too. Also, Manu, the First Man, and Vishnu who became Leviathan. Let's not forget the ocean-warming piglet, either.

One Last Legend

When God commanded certain angels to help him shape a human being in His own image, they were amazed. Yet they joined their efforts to God's play, naturally. As the Bible relates: "On the day that God created Adam, in the likeness of God He created him; male and female He created them."

The Zohar (the Kabbalist Mishnah attributed to Moses de Leon) explains that puzzling passage as follows: "From this we learn that any image which fails to embrace male and female is not a high or true image. The Blessed Holy One does not establish His abode anywhere that male and female are not found together. Blessings are found only where a male and female are found. . . . A human being is called Adam only when male and female are one."

The angels completed their work unquestioningly. But later they asked God to explain why he had caused them to shape Adam in His own image. The Creator replied indirectly, as follows:

First, he asked his angels to name the various plants and animals upon the face of the earth. Although they had assumed active roles in the making of those creatures as well, the angels stood abashed, for they had no names to bestow. Then God called upon the first man, shaped in His own image.

"What is your name?" God asked.

"Adam, meaning of earth."

"And what is my name?" God pursued.

"Adonai, meaning lord of all."

"Very well. Now please name all the fellow-creatures that you see around you here."

Thereupon, Adam gave names to grasses, ferns, flowers, trees, insects, fishes, birds and beasts, finding distinctive words for each and every species in turn. To us, such names are convenient labels. But the first man, who was also the first woman, shaped each one out of silence and sympathy.

Unfathomable Abundance

I'm about to end this book fairly near the place where it began, recalling Camp Mohawk. During my boyhood summer there I made an Indian headdress, the kind that sports a wavy diadem of feathers in front plus lots more trailing down one's back. To tell the truth, my headdress came in a kit. All I had to do was put it together, which I managed rather well. At least Chief Little Fish pronounced himself satisfied. But he said I still had a lot to learn about wearing it. Like standing straighter, to start with.

Actually, Chief Little Fish went on, I ought never to touch the headdress without having prepared myself first. I should wait until I felt peaceful and quiet, "like a soaring bird," he explained, in order to "let the beads and feathers speak."

That never happened in the literal sense, needless to say, but nonetheless I knew what the chief meant. When wearing my Indian headdress I felt safe yet brave at the same time. I became conscious of something that one usually takes for granted. Namely, being in nature. Not only that, but being part of nature, too, in a curiously transparent way. It seemed to me that I could almost hear my beaded blue and yellow headband murmur, while my eagle feathers nodded slightly, whispering amongst themselves!

Anaximenes said that "Air" holds both the cosmos and the individual soul together. In his Cambridge lecture on "The Principle of Objectivation," Erwin Schrödinger suggested something similar. "The world is given but once," he observed. "Nothing is reflected. The original and the mirror-image are identical."

We can't leap out of nature. The same elements that go to make up the universe comprise one's mind; they are identical. As

191

Schrödinger concluded: "This situation is the same for every mind and its world in spite of the unfathomable abundance of cross-references between them."

The universe does indeed encompass an unfathomable abundance of cross-references! Time cannot corrode this abundance, nor will eternity wear it down. The mythosphere lives and shines.

Index